THE
ENGAGEMENT RING
HANDBOOK

A **MAN'S** GUIDE TO GETTING IT RIGHT

R3THINK PRESS

First published in Great Britain 2016
by Rethink Press (www.rethinkpress.com)

CONTENTS

INTRODUCTION

About this book

So, you've decided that the time has come to propose to your beloved. Now all you have to do is find the perfect ring. That's the easy bit – no?

Well you would think so, but buying an engagement ring is rather like buying a high-spec bicycle. Unless you've done your research, when you take your shiny new bike out for its first ride you will discover all the things about riding it that the salesman in the shop never mentioned. You'll be less impressed by its trendy colours and fancy stickers, but you *will* notice how hard it is to ride uphill due to its weight and even on the flat due to the thick off-road tyres that you don't need.

So it is with engagement rings. There are many things you need to know before you make your final decision – you do not want to discover all the problems no-one told you about *after* you have made your purchase and she has the ring on her finger*.

You just want to get it right.

Over the years, I have seen so many people get it wrong. There are lots of reasons why, but they boil down to having incomplete, inaccurate or misleading information. You can do tons of research, gather mountains of data and comment, but you need to be able to evaluate that information and apply it. That usually requires more knowledge and experience than most first time buyers can expect to have.

A keen cyclist will frequently upgrade his or her bike and become an expert on the latest gearing systems or lightweight frames and tyres. You don't make a habit of buying engagement rings, so you are not likely to be an expert in that field, and there's a lot to know.

That is why I have written this book. Not to add to the mountain of data, but to help cut through it and make it as easy and pain-free as possible to find that perfect ring and still keep within your personal budget.

---

* An important note: this book will help anyone who is buying a ring, whatever gender the giver or receiver may be, and whatever the occasion. But it is written very much with my clients in mind, and these are mostly men who want to surprise their girlfriends with the perfect proposal of marriage. For reasons of style I decided not to attempt to make the text gender neutral and I apologise now to readers who find this annoying or alienating.

Over the course of this short book I will answer all of the questions raised over the years by my various clients, including the questions you did not even know you needed to ask. I shall equip you to set your own priorities and make the best decision possible in this most important of purchases.

Start with the summary

The book is easy to use. Chapters begin with a bullet-point summary so you can quickly skim the content and read sections in more depth if you want to know more, and they end with a conclusion so you can see if you have missed anything important.

There is a lot here, but you don't have to read it all at once, or even sequentially. This book is designed so that you can dip into sections as you need them.

What's in the book?

Chapter 1 starts with what you are trying to get done. I outline the ways in which your ability to source a unique and personal ring to delight your fiancée, and get it absolutely right, have expanded beyond what was possible even three or four years ago.

Chapter 2 offers suggestions for those of you who are unsure to help identify her style and gives tips on how to get her ring size right. Chapter 3 addresses setting your budget to ensure you get good value.

Chapters 4 and 5 identify some common mistakes to avoid when buying a ring and where to find advice and guidance you can trust.

In Chapter 6 we look briefly at the background to current traditions in rings to offer a longer perspective on the matter in hand.

Chapter 7 is about the diamond market and ethics, an increasingly important issue for many people, and Chapter 8 covers all the technical stuff you need to know about diamonds. I've left out as much fluff and flummery as possible.

Chapters 9 and 10 are about coloured gemstones and those which are suitable for use in rings to be worn for a lifetime – not all are. Then Chapter 11 looks at precious metals.

Chapters 12 and 13 deal with designing your ring, with illustrations of styles and settings and the finer design points your jeweller should be taking care of for you.

And finally, in Chapter 14 I've included some personal stories of proposals to inspire you for a proposal you will both remember forever.

I'm sure that you will not need everything in this book, and I have no doubt that for some I will have missed things you do want to know. That's another great thing about technology – if there's anything you want to raise, questions you want to ask or comments you want to make, you'll find my contact details at the end of the book.

CHAPTER 1

WHAT DO YOU WANT TO GET DONE?

If you were buying a new car or bike, digital device or piece of sports equipment, you would know what you were looking for in appearance, performance, design, materials, comfort/ergonomics, build quality, expected life, envy factor, price, etc. You would know what you wanted it to do for you.

You are probably already thinking about proposing and may have started researching or looking for that engagement ring. I would hazard a guess that what you want to do is find the perfect ring that will (1) be special and unique to her, which she'll love; (2) show her how much you love her and think of her; (3) do the job and last forever; (4) be beautifully designed and made; and (5) fit within your budget without breaking the bank.

Summary

- You want this ring to be the most special piece of jewellery you ever give, but the engagement ring market is flooded with mass produced designs, and the same rings are given to hundreds of women the world over

- People want more personalisation, not standardisation. New technology has put that within your reach

- You are in control of all the decisions and this makes personalisation potentially the best value option of all

First, set your criteria

The first thing to do is to identify what you already know you want from this ring. This ring must…

Make a note of at least five important things you want this ring to be – what it should do, the key things you want to get right. You may find a lot more than five. Even if it is just a general statement of principle, it's good to get the list out there in the open. It'll start you thinking, and you can test it against new facts and ideas as you come across them.

This is just a start. As you go through the book you'll discover things you didn't know which may introduce a whole new set of possibilities.

Outside the box?

Once you have come up with some general criteria, where do you start your search for this perfect ring? If you've done any research at all you will know there is a lot of information out there, a lot to think about, and plenty of places to look for inspiration.

If you want something original, personal to you both and unique to her then you should think about whether you expect to find it 'off-the-shelf' or hope to have a ring 'designed-for-her'. It may not have been the first question you asked yourself, but it is one you should be open to right at the beginning as your thoughts on that will determine how you go about your search.

Most of my clients start by looking around their local High Street jewellers, Googling 'engagement rings' or visiting the well-known 'jewellery quarters' in Birmingham, London and elsewhere – I examine each of these in Chapter 5. They usually find the options all start to look the same, and that is not what they want. They want something different and personal, but can't find it in these places. They also feel slightly nervous about not taking the 'safe option', so they want to feel comfortable that whatever they choose will be the right thing.

In the past, few people had the opportunity to commission a design just for them. It was too costly and took too long, and the idea still persists that it's an expensive route taking months to complete. Luckily for you, things have changed.

Before we launch into all the other things you might want to know before you buy your engagement ring, let's first examine the idea of a unique design.

Bespoke, Customised and Off-The-Shelf – what is the difference?

The terms 'Bespoke' and 'Custom-made' are often used interchangeably for personalised designs, but there is a difference.

Bespoke. A bespoke ring is designed from scratch and made exclusively for you to a unique design. Like a bespoke suit, it is completely personal and fits your priorities exactly.

The design is created in principle precisely to your specifications, then the diamonds or gemstones are sourced according to your criteria and the final ring is built around your stones to enhance their individual qualities. This is the most personal, flexible way to create a ring.

Custom-made. Custom-making a ring is like selecting your options for a new car. The car may be a mass produced design, but you get to choose the equipment, interior and paint job. When building a custom ring, you choose from a selection of ring mounts and metals then add a standard sized diamond (usually) of your choice. Custom-made is more flexible than a ready-made ring, but it is not a personalised design and usually has few options for alternative gemstones.

Off-the-Shelf. Off-the-shelf or ready-made rings are just that. You see one in a shop or online, and you buy it. This is the least personal option, and the same design will be worn by hundreds of women; the only personal touches you can add are re-sizing it to fit or ordering it in the ring size you want. Ready-mades use standard-spec diamonds, often uncertified (see Chapter 8). You are limited by the stock shops hold, and they have an interest in selling you just what they have, which will not necessarily be what best fits your priorities.

What's new?

Although most people, including jewellers, don't realise it, fantastic developments in technology and software are revolutionising jewellery design and production for clients. It's long been used in industry, but now designers and jewellers have access to the same technology from their studio and laptop and are using it to produce individual designs *with their clients*.

No longer does a designer have to spend many hours creating designs on paper only to have to rework all the detail or some major element over and over again. Excellent new CAD (Computer Aided Design) software has liberated the designer, allowing them to spend time on new and innovative designs instead of laboriously drafting and redrafting the same work.

It's possible to make major real-time changes to a design – *you* can direct the designer to make the changes you want to the finished piece. The ring becomes partly your own creation, adding to its personal story and specialness, which is very exciting.

We all know about the miracle of 3D printers. They can reproduce in fine detail the cellular structures required in complex medical applications. These printers are an example of Computer Aided Manufacture (CAM). The same CAM technology is used with CAD to create intricate, beautiful and robust designs for rings, some of which it would not be possible to make by hand. In the past, incredible filigree work was created by court craftsmen with all the time in the world, producing for princes and bankrolled by national treasuries. Most people's pockets are not that deep, but now that doesn't stop you from having a ring fit for a prince (or a princess, for that matter).

And finally, all of this is achieved in much less time than traditional bespoke manufacture. The designer saves time with CAD, the craftsman saves time with CAM, and the final ring is a more faithful realisation of the original design. This has a massive impact on cost, because these new tools make the specialists in their field more productive and efficient and their time more cost-effective.

In essence, what the new CAD/CAM technology does is allow *anyone who wants one* to have a personal bespoke ring, made to their specifications and to the highest standards of craftsmanship, within both their budget and a few short weeks.

If you can have a unique personal ring that easily and that quickly, why wouldn't you?

Conclusion

You want this ring to be the most special piece of jewellery you will ever give to the woman in your life and you want her to love it. But the engagement ring market is flooded with mass produced standard designs, both in shops and online, and the same rings are given to hundreds of women the world over.

Increasingly people are looking for greater personalisation in the things they use and buy. Bespoke is challenging the supremacy of mass production and offers more people the chance to express their individuality and uniqueness.

Just like choosing the right hi-spec bicycle, finding the right engagement ring to delight her, which is well designed, built to last and within your budget, requires some specialist knowledge. Customisation has been around a while and is fine as far as it goes, but you now have more options than ever before. New technology has put within your reach the exclusivity of a personalised bespoke service and, because you are in control of all the decisions, if you find the right designer this has become the most attractive and best value option of all.

Commissioning a bespoke ring may seem a little daunting at first, and it may take you out of your comfort zone, but the rest of this book will help you to make the right choices. Make the most of this opportunity to truly delight and surprise your fiancée to be.

CHAPTER 2

GETTING IT RIGHT – STYLE AND RING SIZE

An engagement ring may not be the biggest or even the most expensive piece of jewellery you ever give her, but it *is* the one she will wear the longest and remember forever. And when you propose it will be one of the most significant and memorable events in your lives together. Getting it right is all down to preparation.

Summary

- To find the perfect ring you need to understand her style and know what she loves. It's all about the thought that goes into it, not how much you spend

- Get the ring size as nearly correct as possible – there are ways to do this and tools to help

- Many rings can be resized, but some designs cannot and would have to be completely remade. You need to know which is which – if not for now, then for the future

- In the end, the success of the final result depends upon excellent preparation.

Knowing her style

When you really start to look at rings you might conclude that making a decision on the right one is almost as hard as deciding who you want to marry. Getting a handle on her style and what she likes is the key. We all know how hard it is, and we appreciate the thought and care you put into it far more than any amount of money you might spend.

Many of you will have a very clear idea of what your partner likes and wants. If that's you, skip to the section on ring sizes right now.

For those of you who are less sure, here are some ideas.

Research Tips. There are three levels of research which may require increasing degrees of subterfuge:

Level 1 – Basic. Check out her wardrobe. You could casually compliment her on what she's wearing, ask her where she got it and why she likes it. *Or* you could offer to take her for lunch and a shopping trip one Saturday. Take photos on your phone of the things she tries on. For that matter, take more photos in general, especially when you go out together. They will create a visual record of the colours she wears and the styles she favours.

Does she have a different style of clothes for work and play? Look at what she does actually wear – some of her wardrobe may never see the light of day.

Level 2 – Intermediate. Take a good look at any of the social media she shares. Pinterest is a very useful social media resource where people gather and share images of the things they love. Women use it a lot, men less so, but it's a great place to collect design ideas, whether for a ring or a new building project. If you can, you should find a reason to get her to show you her Pinterest boards, or any other social media she may use to share ideas. Do they reflect her values and the things she cares about, whether it's saving the planet or the latest from the catwalks? Is there a clothes designer she loves but maybe can't afford? Look at her ideas for interior design and decoration.

Level 3 – Tricky. If you can, take a look in her jewellery box, or make a point of noticing what sort of jewellery she wears – photos are useful here again. We all have some old jewellery which is only of sentimental value. Does she wear silver or gold, plain or full of colour? Is her jewellery small and dainty, or big and bold? Does she like traditional or modern; simple or elaborate; conservative or flamboyant? Does she wear much jewellery at all?

Aim to get a feel for her overall style. The more you look at what she loves and actually wears, the more you will develop an instinctive feel for her style, and the more confidence you will have in your choice of ring.

Research Checklist

If you'd like a structured approach to the task of research, use the link to download your 'What's her Style' checklist to record her style and preferences.

www.juliepeel.co.uk/Downloads/HerStyle

As long as you update it every so often, not only will it help you decide on the right ring now, it will also help with many other decisions in the future. You'll never be lost for ideas for birthday, anniversary and other special occasion gifts.

Getting the size right

Sometimes finding out her ring size is the trickiest question of all. If you want the whole proposal to be a complete surprise, you may have to resort to subterfuge to answer this one. There are ways to get round the problem, which I will outline first, followed by an explanation of the technicalities of getting her size right.

You may already know her ring size from previous experience, which would be very helpful. Or you may have to play detective. Whatever you do, make sure you are getting a measurement for the correct finger *and* you are absolutely sure which finger you have a measurement for.

'Borrow' a Ring. If you can, 'acquire' a ring which you *know* she wears from her jewellery box. This is a good start, but make absolutely sure you know for certain (a) that she still wears it, and (b) which *hand* and which *finger* she wears it on. If she wears it on the ring finger of her right hand, she's right-handed and it fits well, it is probably about a half to a full size too large for her left hand. Your ring size will need to be adjusted accordingly.

The wrong finger

Andy B was adamant that his partner wore the ring he'd 'borrowed' on the ring finger of her right hand. So I made adjustments by one size, but it did seem quite large for the woman he'd described.

Well, she loved her ring. But I had to reduce it *four whole sizes*, which is a lot for any design, because in fact she wore the ring he'd borrowed on her middle finger – much larger than the ring finger.

It is not always possible to make such drastic changes without remodelling the ring completely, so it's worth taking extra care to get the size as near as possible.

The best friend option. Another ruse is to enlist the help of your future fiancée's girlfriend, with the obvious caveat that she be super trustworthy. On the pretence of looking for a ring for herself, she can find out all sorts of useful information if they go 'window shopping' together.

A little help from her friend

Ian C's sister Amanda was not only very friendly with his girlfriend, she was also hoping to be engaged in the near future. So Ian asked Amanda to take his girlfriend with her when she went window shopping for rings. (He even supplied the champagne lunch to make it more fun.) The information he got from that trip was priceless in terms of helping with the design of his girlfriend's ring, and we went for a yellow sapphire with diamonds, which he would not otherwise have considered. That champagne lunch turned out to be a very good investment.

An Educated Guess. An experienced jewellery designer should be able to take an educated guess at your fiancée's ring size from a photograph of her. A full profile photo, together with a close up of her hands if possible, is most useful. Even if you have managed to purloin a ring, this can help confirm the estimate. It may not be a perfect size, but it is better to get it approximately right than completely wrong.

Every picture tells a story

Kieran described the love of his life as 'short and quite cuddly' and estimated her ring size at about N. He took some photos with his phone when they were at a family party, and as a result I could see that she had beautiful small hands with fine fingers much nearer to a size J. So we went for J1/2, and luckily her ring fitted perfectly.

Ring and finger measuring tools. You can get a gadget (like a moveable tie-wrap with letters on it) to help you estimate her ring size, and there are sizing cards to measure ring diameters.

Neither is infallible, but again, better than nothing. The only way to be absolutely sure is to measure her finger with a professional ring gauge, but that is not an option when it's to be a surprise.

You can download a couple of practical tools from my website, including instructions on how best to use them, here:

www.juliepeel.co.uk/downloads/ringsizetools

and request a free ring sizing gadget to be sent by post – be sure to use the reference 'BOOK1' and include a postal address.

Email: info@juliepeel.co.uk

If all else fails. It is not the end of the world if you get her size wrong. Most engagement rings can be resized, and if you are having it made for you, the designer should warn you if resizing will be a problem.

Resizing is only really tricky if there is filigree, an applied or engraved design around the whole circumference, shank stones in claw settings or on more than half the shank. Then the ring might have to be partially rebuilt to make it larger or smaller, which may be costly.

Generally speaking, for a more straightforward band it is easier to make a ring smaller than it is to make it larger. When it is done properly, resizing always requires cutting, shaping, soldering and re-polishing the ring. So it is easier and less expensive to take a bit out than it is to add metal, especially if there is engraving, stones or an applied design on the band.

Understanding ring sizing

Sizing Conventions. In the UK, ring sizes are denoted by letters from A to Z, and beyond. There are different sizing conventions in the US, Continental Europe, the Antipodes and elsewhere.

A standard UK ring size for women is around M or N, with H being very small and S being at the larger end. A lot of women, especially younger women, might have ring sizes of J to L. For men, standard sizes are around R and S, size P for slim hands, and greater than Z is possible.

It is worth knowing that the difference in diameter over one full size is less than *half a millimetre*, and half a size can make a big difference to the fit of a ring, especially if it has a large stone (as it will turn more readily). This is why using a piece of string or wool is not going to work as a measuring tool!

Measuring Size. There are two principle ways to measure the size of a ring (as opposed to the finger). These are (a) to the leading edge, and (b) to the mid-point. The first measures the ring size at the point where the edge of the ring will go no further down the sizing stick. The second measures the size at the point of the middle of the ring shank on the stick. Given the small tolerance on size diameters, this difference can be significant, especially for wider rings.

Wide rings typically need to be larger than narrow rings to fit properly over the knuckle and sit on the finger comfortably without squeezing the fleshy bit into the finger-equivalent of a 'muffin top'. This also applies when a group of rings is worn on one finger.

A third consideration is the fact that fingers do go up and down in size during the day and depending on the weather. If you measure her finger on a hot summer's day, it could be out by a whole size or more.

Just be aware of these factors if you do get a finger measurement.

Which Hand? In the UK, engagement rings and wedding bands are worn on the ring finger of the left hand, with the wedding band on first, followed by the engagement ring and any eternity rings, but customs vary internationally. For example, in Spain, wedding rings are worn on the right hand.

For a right handed person, the fingers on the right hand are usually slightly larger – a half to a full size – than those on the left, and vice versa for a left handed person. So this will influence how you measure for the hand you need.

Conclusion

Doing the background research on her style and the correct ring size is something only you can do, and it is the first and most important step in getting her ring just right. This is true whether you are buying a ring off-the-shelf or having one made, and it is the one crucial step which people often miss out.

Preparation is key, and there are tools to help. Whether it is in sport, in business or just redecorating the house, the success of the final result depends upon the preparation.

CHAPTER 3

ABOUT THE MONEY

One of the Big Questions for most men buying an engagement ring is 'How much should I spend?' And, whenever I am asked this question, my answer is always the same – spend only what you are comfortable with. A key message of this whole book is to set your own parameters; there are no rules. *Do not spend more money on this ring than you can afford, or want to spend.*

Think creatively about financing, set some realistic expectations and go for quality over quantity. Last of all, don't forget the insurance.

Summary

- You, and only you, should decide what you want to spend on your ring. Ignore salary-based 'rules' – it's all just marketing

- Go for quality over quantity and set your expectations realistically – designers are not magicians but there are ways to design around budgets

- Think about financing and factor in financing costs

- Check your insurance options – a general policy may not be the best choice.

The 'Two Months' Salary rule' and the power of marketing

You may have heard people say that you should spend about two months' salary on an engagement ring. Some people think it's 'traditional'. But, if you think about it, it hardly makes any sense at all, as one person's two months' salary might be another's annual wage packet.

It started in the 1930s as 'one month's salary' in an advertising campaign designed to rescue the De Beers company from disaster following the Great Depression. In the 1980s it became two months' worth, but in Japan in the 1970s De

Beers had ramped it up to three, taking advantage of the Japanese concepts of honour and saving face. Far from being a tradition, these 'salary rules' are an adman's confection.

For over a century, until the 1990s when they started to lose exclusive control of supply, the De Beers cartel controlled the diamond market. They first created the perception that only a diamond would do to express your undying love, and then that it was expected you should spend a substantial proportion of your hard earned salary on it. I hope that these facts put those particular myths into perspective.

Set *your* budget

So yes, this ring is very important, but she will value even more the care and attention you put into finding her a unique ring she will love. You need to feel happy about what you are spending on it. This is not being unromantic or parsimonious, it is purely practical.

You do not want to wake up the next day, next week, or next year, and regret having spent too much money on a piece of jewellery. Worse still, if you ever resent the expense, she will notice. Giving freely with love is an even better feeling than receiving, so you have to be entirely happy about it. Apart from anything else, you don't want to be in hock to the bank years later or when there is a wedding and a honeymoon to be paid for too.

Peter's story

I had a very inventive client who knew just what sort of ring his girlfriend wanted. He wanted her to have that ring, but he did not have the budget to pay for it, and the plan was that they would be getting married just a few months after he proposed. He could see a lot of expense down the line, but he also wanted her to have the best he could afford. For them this meant that it was going to be platinum and diamonds all the way.

Being a practical man, he had a great solution to this. I designed exactly the ring she wanted, which included a big diamond surrounded by smaller stones, and we made the ring in platinum with all the little diamonds in the halo and down the shank – *but* the wheeze was we put a large cubic zirconium (fake diamond) in the middle.

This was all done in secret. When he proposed she was bowled over and loved the ring. He did tell her what he had done, and that the plan was to buy the diamond to go in the middle on their first wedding anniversary, when he had saved up enough to pay for that too. She was thrilled and thought that was a great way to do it; they didn't tell anyone else, and no-one knew or guessed.

So everyone was really happy. She got the ring she wanted, he could afford to pay for it, her mum was super impressed and no-one was any the wiser!

What you spend on your ring has to fit in with your values as well as your bank balance. It is something which will last forever, so it is probably worth going for quality over quantity, or at least recognising that you can't get a silk purse of a ring for a sow's ear of cash. Always set your priorities and be honest with yourself and realistic about what is possible. If your budget is limited and she wants a humungous rock then it all might have to wait a while.

So, before you go looking, decide how much you want to spend and write it down. Do not allow this figure to creep up, no matter how persuasive the salesperson or how beautiful the ring. Set your budget in stone and get the best you can within that limit.

How to pay? – factor in the financing

There will be a lot more expenses to think about over the next couple of years after she has said 'Yes'. There will probably be a wedding to plan and save for, you may be saving for a deposit on a place of your own, or even planning a family. So think carefully about the future and the best way to pay for your ring in the medium term.

This is likely to be a significant expense on anyone's scale, and although we are used to paying for larger items on our credit cards, if you can't pay off the card in a very short time it is an expensive way to finance your purchase. At the time of writing, banks typically charge 16%–25% interest per year on credit card balances, and perhaps a bit less for overdrafts or loans.

Some retailers offer financing arrangements, even 0% financing arrangements, but credit financing is expensive for retailers too. If it sounds too good to be true, it usually is – that 0% deal will already have been factored into the price of your ring.

To offer any form of credit arrangements legally, even to refer a client to a financing organisation, the retailer has to be registered under the Consumer Credit Acts. This is designed to protect people from themselves, but as an unintended consequence it does disadvantage the smaller independents. Registration is an expensive and uncertain business so many smaller retailers and designers are unable to offer this service to their customers, however much they would like to.

If you are thinking of using a credit card, an overdraft, a loan or any other form of financing, you need to know how much interest you will pay because that is part of the cost of your ring. If you have a budget of £3,000 and you will be charged £500 interest while you pay off the financing, you only have £2,500 left to spend on the ring. And even if you keep reducing the balance, interest accrues on all your purchases, not just on the old balances. If you are saving for a wedding, a home or a family, how will those repayments impact on your future plans?

There are of course credit card deals where you are not charged interest for the first six months or so, but these are fast disappearing. Clearly they are designed to get you hooked into that provider so that you end up paying their inflated standard interest rate in the end. But if you know that you can pay the ring off in six months, or however long the deal lasts, and you know you are pretty disciplined about those sort of things, then that could be a good option for you.

It may seem a bit old fashioned in our culture of instant gratification, but you might decide to save up until you have enough to pay for the whole thing, or most of it, before you propose. That could mean putting off your engagement for a while, but at least you won't have the expense hanging over you after the event. It will also give you time to do your research and plan just exactly how you are going to propose to make it that truly memorable event. After all, if you are going to spend the rest of your lives together, maybe a few months of saving up isn't the end of the world.

Quality vs price

Whatever you do, don't make the mistake of compromising on the key elements which are of greatest importance to you just to save a couple of hundred pounds. Make savings elsewhere in the wedding plans – flowers last a day, this ring is for life.

Cutting corners on the important stuff is one of the key mistakes people make when buying a ring, so I have devoted Chapter 4 to precisely that subject – the common key mistakes.

Insurance

This seems as good a place as any to remind you about the important matter of insuring your ring as soon as you have purchased it. Choose your jewellery insurer carefully. Adding it to your household policy is not always the best option, and it is well worth considering a specialist jewellery insurer.

Most household insurance policies have a limit on the value of any single item, so if the value of your ring exceeds that limit you would be as well to take out specialist insurance. Your jeweller may offer a service or be able to recommend a good company, otherwise they are easily located online.

Many general insurance companies use the large jewellery chains when settling claims for lost or stolen jewellery. They do this because they have negotiated a discount with those suppliers. This is why claimants are often pressurised into using that chain to replace their lost valuables. If you want to be able to replace your ring with an exact replica in the unfortunate event that it is lost, do check the terms your general insurer will offer before you add your ring to your policy. If you do not agree to use the specified jewellery chain to replace your ring, you will probably find that your general insurance company will reduce any financial settlement by at least 20% of the insured value. If you insist with them on using your own designer or independent retailer to replace a lost bespoke item they will attempt to negotiate the same discount with that supplier and you may end up having to pay the difference.

In my experience, specialist jewellery insurers do not do this. As long as you have proper valuation documentation from your original jeweller or designer at the time of purchase and have kept your valuation for insurance purposes up to date, specialist insurers are less likely to quibble, faster at settling the claim and more accommodating about replacing your lost items with exact replicas, especially if they are bespoke designs.

A lost ring

I designed a very unusual engagement ring for James to give to his fiancée in the spring of 2013, and she really loved it. But while on a beach holiday before their wedding in 2015 she lost it one evening walking back to their hotel. She was devastated, but it could not be found.

I always keep my clients' design files, so it was a simple matter to create an exact replica of the ring she had lost. I could source the same quality and size of sapphires and an equivalent central diamond. The ring was insured under James's general insurance – the only problem was that the price of gemstones had gone up.

Before commissioning the replacement, James wanted to be sure his insurance company would cover the cost. In short, they wouldn't. James had not updated the insured value of his ring, and although his policy stated replacement cost, his insurance company would only honour that if he went to one of their approved suppliers who would not be able to recreate the exact ring they had lost. The best he could achieve was a cash payment of just 80% of the insured value. So, even if gem prices had not risen, he would have had to supplement his insurance settlement to fund the replacement ring. To add insult to injury, they also increased his premiums. Needless to say, James changed insurers at the first opportunity.

Conclusion

The theme of this chapter is that you, and only you, should decide what you want to spend on your ring. So-called traditional rules of one or two months' salary were created by advertising campaigns and should be treated accordingly.

Set your own budget and stick to it. There are inventive and creative ways to achieve what you want without taking you out of your comfort zone, but you do need to be realistic about what can be achieved. Consider a two-stage option if the budget doesn't match the aspiration at this stage – there will always be anniversaries when you could upgrade.

Think about how you are going to finance the purchase, and factor any financing costs into the total or it could end up being an expensive purchase for what you are actually getting.

On the subject of things financial, do check your insurance options thoroughly as well. Just adding your ring to your existing household insurance may not be the best way to do it. You might find that a company that specialises in insuring jewellery offers better cover if you do have the misfortune to lose the ring or damage a stone. General insurers have exclusive deals with the multiples in which *they* get a discount; specialist insurers are more likely to pay the full cost of replacing a designed ring with an exact replica.

CHAPTER 4

SOME COMMON MISTAKES AND MISCONCEPTIONS

For most people, an engagement ring is a once in a lifetime purchase, so they have no experience of what it involves or what they need to think about and be aware of. There are many areas where they know they need more information (the known unknowns), but the most dangerous territory is the 'unknown unknowns', i.e. those things that you don't even know you need to know about.

In this chapter I will highlight some of the most common misconceptions and mistakes I've seen people make which I hope to correct and dispel in the rest of the book.

Summary

- Many myths about engagement rings are peddled as facts. Most are created by ad men, but the 'unknown unknowns' are the most dangerous

- Diamonds are neither rare nor precious. They command high prices because supply is artificially restricted

- Think ahead to the shape of the wedding band. Don't buy on looks and don't assume vintage rings have been repaired

- Beware of 'buying the box', i.e. getting poor value from a big brand

- If it seems too good (cheap) to be true, it probably is. There is a lot of room for opinion when valuing and grading

- Don't leave it all to the last minute, you'll buy under duress

- An engagement ring is not a financial investment

- Doing-it-yourself can lead to poor choices and end up costing you more.

Believing the myths

Do you think that diamonds are rare, precious and special? Or that only diamonds are forever? These are a small sample of the powerful myths about engagement rings, the product of very clever marketing campaigns designed to sell. Don't feel pressurised by false 'traditions' into making choices you otherwise would not make, and don't let these myths, and many more like them, get in the way of what is right for you and your partner.

Not rare and not precious

You wouldn't think it from the way people talk about them, but diamonds are one of the commonest gemstones around. If all the available fully-finished gem-quality diamonds were released to the market tomorrow, the price would drop like a stone and the bottom would fall out of the diamond market completely. That is why supply is so rigidly controlled.

Diamonds are very hard and, properly cut, very sparkly, but they are not rare and, unless a major currency adopts a 'Diamond Standard', they do not have any significant intrinsic value.

So, fashion, marketing and the control of supply creates confidence and keeps the diamond market afloat. If they were suddenly to go out of fashion, or too many diamonds were put up for sale, a lot of people would lose a lot of money. This is one of the reasons the industry is concerned about the successful efforts to grow high quality diamonds cost-effectively in a laboratory. Supply will increase, perhaps prices will normalise and they will lose control of the market. This is happening now and the industry is coming to a very slow and grudging acceptance of laboratory grown diamonds and other gemstones.

Relying on Google

When you don't know where to begin, Google is a great place to do some background research and start to get a feel for your subject, but don't rely on it exclusively or too heavily. The Internet can be as much a source of disinformation as fact.

You'll find all the myths presented as facts somewhere online. There is far too much information to digest, some of it is conflicting or confusing, and Googling won't answer the questions you don't know you need to ask. Remember – most of what you will read online about engagement rings is written by people with an interest in selling them.

Think of your own profession, industry or specialist hobby. If you are an expert in that field, would you recommend anyone to make a key decision based only on what they could glean from Googling your subject?

Making poor choices

This is linked to the last two points, and happens if you try to do it all yourself and don't know enough about what you are buying.

It includes getting the metals wrong, compromising on the wrong things, making a decision based only on the price, not getting good value in your diamond or gemstone, choosing a style or stone which isn't robust enough, won't last or won't work with her lifestyle, and not thinking how it will fit with the wedding ring. All of these, and more, can be avoided, especially if you set your priorities and budget.

The problem with vintage

Beautiful as they can be, vintage rings by definition have been around, and probably worn, for quite a long time. Ring settings and claws show wear and damage, shanks wear thin at the back, diamonds and gemstones get scuffed on the facets or chipped at the edges. Old stones will not be certified, so you have no guarantee about what you are buying, and the ring may not originally have been designed to be worn with a wedding band.

These are all things which it is easy to overlook, or just not see if you do not know what to look for.

You are buying a ring to last and be worn for a lifetime. A vintage ring may already have been worn for a lifetime. Over the years I have had to recreate completely a number of vintage rings which had not been refurbished by the retailer and were sold to unsuspecting clients who did not know what they were buying. I've replaced stones and shanks, created replica settings and, in some cases, complete replica rings because the whole thing was too delicate and damaged to wear. In these cases the rings ended up costing a lot more than if they had simply been made from new.

This does not mean that you should avoid all vintage rings, but you really do need to know what you are buying, what it is really worth and how much refurbishment it will need.

Leaving it to the last minute

If you are reading this, you probably won't be someone who leaves everything to the last minute, but it's easy to spend ages thinking about the ring, preparing for it and not actually getting round to doing anything about it until the last minute.

It's a crass generalisation, but men have a reputation with we women for leaving things like this to the last minute. You may have been planning the proposal for months – the holiday, the dinner, how you'll surprise her – but you haven't quite got around to the ring. Never mind – there are lots out there, right?

Well there are, but you'll be surprised how much they all look alike, and you can't find the right thing, and time is slipping away. As the most important piece of jewellery you will ever buy her, you will not want to rush it. Take your time, plan ahead, but also *do* something about it, and allow *at least* a month if you are having a ring made for you.

Cutting a 'deal'

In this age of the Internet we've got used to shopping around, searching for bargains and good deals. But we may overlook the fact there are things you can't cut corners on, and if something seems incredible value or too good to be true, then it probably is.

Check out the sources of anyone supplying your ring and don't assume that you can cut the price without compromising on quality.

Not such a great deal

A couple became my clients because they needed her ring to be remade. They thought they'd had a very good deal from a well-known jewellery centre in London, but within a couple of weeks, Katherine had problems with the ring: one of its little stones fell out of the shank, the band was too tight, and when it was resized the setting was damaged and the jewellers distorted the whole band shape. It was all a bit of a disaster, Katherine was distraught and did not want to go back to where they had bought it.

When I examined it, the ring was in a poor shape and would not have lasted long, so I completely remade it and reset new stones in the new shank. Katherine was finally happy, but it had cost Richard a lot more than it would have without the 'deal'.

Your ring as an investment

It may be an emotional investment in your future together, but do not ever think of jewellery as a financial investment, unless you are a latter-day Richard Burton. People are perhaps understandably confused about this because they see the insurance value as somehow representing intrinsic or market value. It does not. It represents how much you would have to ask the insurance company for if you wanted to replace the ring with an exact replica.

First of all, an investment is only a financial benefit if it is realised, i.e. *sold*. Under what circumstances do you think you might 'realise' the value of her engagement ring? This one is intended for life, is it not?

Secondly, the 'value' of second-hand jewellery really does come down simply to how much someone is prepared to pay for it on the day. Unless it's a 'vintage' item, many people have an emotional objection to buying a ring which may have come from a relationship break-down, or perhaps because the answer was no.

As long as the stone is in good condition on a second-hand ring, and it may not be, jewellers are the main purchasers. They will dismount the stones for reuse and send the metal for scrap. The same jeweller can buy a new diamond, in perfect condition, together with its original certificate from their diamond dealer at wholesale prices. They will not pay even that for a second hand diamond, which may need repolishing or re-cutting and might also have to be recertified.

So, choose your stones to wear and look beautiful, then invest in a vintage Bugatti if you must.

Conclusion

The list of potential errors is long. This chapter outlines just a few of the areas where people can make mistakes or be misled by myths and misconceptions. The rest of this book will arm you with the information, confidence and resources you need to avoid them all.

CHAPTER 5

WHO DO YOU TRUST?

OK, so you've done your research on her style, you know how much you want to spend, you are aware of the common mistakes (and you're not going to make them), but before you dive in, you need to identify where to go for the best advice and information for *your* needs.

As I said before, there is a lot of information out there. Some is good, but quite a bit of it is either misleading, conflicting or just irrelevant to the real job in hand, which is to find the perfect engagement ring for the person with whom you want to spend the rest of your life. So, how will you know who to trust?

Summary

- With so much information, you need a trustworthy filter and interpreter

- High street chains, jewellery quarters and high-end brands have the substantial costs of capital investment in stock, advertising and premises, for which you will pay

- Their products are standardised, mass produced and of variable quality

- Buying expensive jewellery online is always a gamble

- Independents have a local reputation to maintain and an interest in long term client relationships

- Trust works both ways.

The obvious places

As a man buying an expensive and important piece of fine jewellery for the first time, you may feel a bit like a lamb going for slaughter, or at least somewhat confused. What you want is expert advice, so where do you go to find an expert? Well, you go to the obvious places, because those are the only ones you know about.

The obvious places include locations like London's Hatton Garden, the Birmingham Jewellery Quarter, Glasgow's Argyle Arcade, the High Street chains, Tiffany, Cartier or other big brands, and, of course, our good friend Google.

These are fine for general research, but you can be overwhelmed with 'diamond ring fatigue'. Many of my clients have suffered just that before they come to me. In total desperation to get the whole thing over and done with, you could end up falling for the pitch of the next persuasive sales person. Whatever you do, do *not* succumb. Do not buy from any of these places unless, and until, you truly know what you want, and what you are doing.

Jewellery quarters and High Street chains

So, what are the issues with the obvious places? Well, stock for one thing, staff sales incentives for another, and relative anonymity for a third. These are all linked. Unlike most independent jewellers, many of these retail outlets do not expect you to be a repeat customer so they have no incentive to consider your immediate interests over their own.

Stock and the cost of capital. The obvious places carry masses of valuable stock (inventory). Stock ties up capital. We all know that capital has a cost in the form of interest, and this applies to all the capital invested in a business.

Think about how much you are charged for a bank loan. Guess who pays in the end for all that money tied up in a company's inventory? This is a really old fashioned and inefficient way to supply jewellery. It does not add to the value of your ring, and with the wonders of modern technology it doesn't have to be like this.

Sales incentives and commissions. Retail staff in most jewellery companies are paid sales commission. Unless there is a commitment to building long term client relationships, their interest is to sell you the ring which will generate the biggest commission or the most personal benefit for them. Surprisingly, this may not necessarily be the most expensive ring. Because holding stock is an expensive business, the greatest benefit to the sales person might be to shift a ring which has been sitting in stock for ages because no-one wants to buy it.

Sales staff are often given extra price flexibility and an added incentive over their normal commission rates to sell that immovable object. Saturdays are favourite days for this tactic, and staff are trained to be brilliant at it. This practice is not confined to the jewellery industry, but it is common within it.

Anonymity, customer relationships and trust. In retail, as in most business, the most important objective should be to build a long term relationship of trust with your client or customer. The objective is one of mutual benefit – the client receives exceptional service and an excellent product and in turn becomes a loyal customer, referring friends, family and even strangers. So a good jeweller wouldn't palm you off with old stock just to get rid of it. If not *your* future business (which they would of course hope to secure through trust and good service), a local or independent jeweller has a wider reputation to think of and would not jeopardise this hard won asset for a quick engagement ring sale.

The big brands

OK, what about Tiffany, Cartier and the other big brands? They do have reputations to maintain.

I agree. So what's the problem there?

As well as their reputations, they are keen to make their product appear exclusive and somehow even more special. How do they achieve that? Well, they spend a small fortune on PR, brand awareness, lifestyle advertising, and premises in prime retail locations. And, in the words of the old Stella Artois adverts, they keep their prices 'reassuringly expensive' – a strategy employed by all 'high-end' brands from lagers to limousines. For Tiffany and the rest, the high prices in part are necessary to pay for all the PR, advertising, premises and also to provide returns to their shareholders, but mostly they keep their prices high to create the illusion of exclusivity. Does this add any value to your ring? I don't think so.

You will undoubtedly get a good quality ring from Tiffany, Cartier and the like. You would not expect otherwise. But this is *not* like comparing an Aston Martin, Mercedes or Rolls Royce with a Ford, VW or Toyota. When you buy a high-end car as opposed to a good mid-range vehicle, you know you are getting extras. The design, the build quality, the appearance, the 'cachet', (the insurance!) and everything about an Aston Martin One–77 (only seventy-seven ever built), for example, is remarkable, special and identifiably different. And it will continue to be so for as long as you own it, and beyond. No-one else can produce the same car with the same qualities, and that is part of what you are paying for.

This is not the case with diamond rings. Diamonds are standardised commodities, graded by a variety of certifying organisations of which the GIA (Gemmological Institute of America) is most respected. As I will reveal later, there is nothing very special about diamonds compared to other precious stones. Even for the best quality diamonds, excluding named monsters like the Krupps or Taylor-Burton, there are always others which would be completely indistinguishable and interchangeable in an engagement ring. Any single one carat D colour VS1 clarity brilliant ideal cut GIA certified diamond (see Chapter 8 for what all *that* gobbledegook means) looks pretty much like another to everyone but the specialist, especially when set in a fairly generic 6-claw solitaire ring mount (Chapter 13).

And that is what you get. As much as any of the High Street chains and online bargain engagement ring websites, all the brands have their standard designs. They are not exclusive, they are not limited and they are not particularly special. Anyone can buy that ring design, and many other makers produce almost exactly the same thing. If you look at Tiffany's website in particular, it offers pretty ordinary rings. They are well made, but there is nothing about them to justify a premium over any other well-made engagement ring of the same technical specification. They may have the maker's name engraved inside, but the extra you spend on the name does not add anything to the 'value' of your ring. After all, she doesn't wear the pretty blue branded box on her finger, and it's not quite the done thing to remind everyone you meet that your ring is from 'X'.

Bargain online retailers

In which case, maybe you are thinking, I should just run an online search on 'engagement rings', buy from one of the big sellers and be done with it. For the bargain hunters among you, if you are not looking for something personal or individual, one of the big online diamond ring companies may be your final destination – *but read this first.*

They are certainly cheaper than the brands. Their mounts are standard and mass produced with options for different stone sizes, and their business models enable them to offer a long list of diamonds. This is because they do not hold the stones themselves, but act as resellers for their partner diamond merchants. They often require their partner to supply these diamonds exclusively to them so that customers cannot compare the same diamond at another price on another website and have an independent means of verifying the quality of the stone or its market value.

There has also been some significant concern in the industry about 'over-certification' (see Chapter 8). This is where diamonds are certified as being substantially better than they really are. In my opinion, this is an inevitable consequence of the way online selling has developed and the commoditisation of diamonds. But it is not a problem only online retailers encounter.

It would always be wise, if taking the online option, to go for a higher specification diamond than you think you need, particularly in relation to cut and clarity (Chapter 8). This is because there are different standards, even for certified diamonds, and as you usually do not have even a photograph of what you are buying, you cannot gauge the stone's brilliance, symmetry, cut or whether or not it is 'eye clean'. Nor can you know if you are comparing like with like when looking at online prices vs your local independent jeweller.

One of the biggest online diamond engagement ring companies doesn't make the product it sells, doesn't see the diamond before it is set or the finished ring before it is shipped to you. The diamond can be supplied in one country, shipped directly to the manufacturer in another country, then the ring is sent on to you in the packaging of the online company from which you bought it. Rarely do you get to see a photograph of the actual diamond itself before you buy it, although you can view the certificate it comes with. You can always return the ring if you are not happy with it, but even when you have got it in your hands, you are unlikely to be able to appraise the stone yourself (which takes years of training and experience).

Online companies will provide appraisals (valuations) for their rings. These always 'value' the ring higher, sometimes much higher, than the price you paid for it as they have a vested interest in making you think your ring is 'worth' more than you paid for it. On the face of it, this appraisal is for insurance purposes, and partly because of the way the insurance industry works, insurance values are sometimes inflated (see Chapter 3). Such an appraisal is simply one person's opinion of how much it might cost you to replace that same article with another identical ring; it does not reflect the 'value' of your ring – and the value of any jewellery is a moveable concept at the best of times. If the valuation is too high, you will be paying too much in insurance premiums, which is not helpful if you are on a budget, however good it makes you feel to believe you have a ring 'worth' more than you paid for it.

Buying any jewellery online is a gamble as you have no way of telling the real quality of the article until you hold it in your hand, and corners are often cut to keep prices down. It works for some people and not for others, as the wide range of satisfaction levels in online reviews attest. As with anything, if it seems too good to be true, it usually is.

So who *do* you trust?

Personally, I would do my basic research and then find an independent jeweller I can talk to. These are the specialists in their field – they care about their subject, have studied it for years and know it inside out. Many have a bricks and mortar base, so you 'know where they live', and they have a reputation to maintain. They often also operate online, conducting personal consultations using Skype and other 'face time' applications.

You don't have to spend hours on appointments, or make excuses to explain where you are going. With the use of screen sharing to discuss design options and CAD renders, you can see what the finished ring will actually look like. New technology offers great potential for jewellers and, if they are embracing it as independents, you will get the best of both worlds. It brings bespoke within the reach of most people in the market for an engagement ring. The designs are created exclusively for you, so you get to choose the stones, set your priorities and determine your own budget. And an independent bespoke designer will offer much better value than a brand, *plus* she won't be wearing the same ring as thousands of other women.

Remember, though, that trust works both ways. Be straightforward and honest with your jeweller and expect the same in return. You can let them know that you have done your research, discuss your priorities, their designs and ethos, then see what they can offer.

Many designers put considerable creative time and effort into each client enquiry. You should not expect them to 'match' the cheap online ring suppliers on price; you are paying for originality, and you have no way of knowing if you would be comparing like with like anyway (see above re price comparisons). If you are only interested in the price you can always buy online and take your chances.

But if you want something more than that – something of good value, better than the standard model, a guarantee of quality, good customer service, ethical sourcing and perhaps even a personal design, all of these are available from independent jewellers using modern design and production technology, whether they operate in your local High Street, online or both.

Conclusion

There is potential for information overload so you need a trustworthy filter and interpreter. High Street chains, jewellery quarters and high-end brands have similar costs of capital investment in stock, advertising and premises, etc. Some of these have little interest in developing lasting client relationships so have no incentive to put the client first. Products are at best standardised and at worst of poor quality. And buying expensive jewellery online is always a gamble.

An independent jeweller has a reputation to maintain and an interest in developing a long term relationship with clients. If they also offer the latest in design and manufacturing technology, the client can benefit in all ways from the reduced overheads and increased choice and flexibility that bespoke design offers.

CHAPTER 6

A VERY BRIEF HISTORY

There is an assumption, in many Western cultures anyway, that if a couple gets engaged, there has to be a ring. But have you ever stopped to think about how we got to where we are now? A bit of background may give you some food for thought about your own symbol of commitment.

Summary

- Rings have been used for millennia as significant cultural symbols, but the popular concept of an engagement ring is a relatively recent invention

- The idea of spending 15% of your annual income on a diamond ring is a marketing construct, but it became the 'safe bet' for many men

- In the twenty-first century the 'rules' have changed – there aren't any. Many people choose more personal symbols of their commitment.

- The 'easy' option (for some) of a diamond ring is not the safe bet it once was

- If a ring is the thing, men need to think more creatively when choosing it.

When did it start?

The engagement or betrothal ring has been around a very long time. To the Egyptians, the circle was the symbol of eternity. The hole in the centre represented a gateway to the future, so a ring was an expression of everlasting love. The Romans used two plain bands – iron for wearing at home and engraved gold for public appearances.

The first documented diamond engagement ring was Archduke Maximillian's betrothal to Mary of Burgundy in 1477. In the sixteenth century the wedding ring was the primary symbol associated with marriage, and betrothal rings were uncommon until the nineteenth century. Even then, the ring presented to Queen Victoria by Prince Albert was a simple affair in the form of a snake with emerald eyes – snakes being a symbol of eternal love, and emerald being Victoria's birthstone.

Diamonds are forever? Only since 1947

The modern idea that a proposal of marriage is not a proper proposal without a diamond engagement ring, on which you may have spent more than 15% of your net annual income, doesn't go back any further than the mid-twentieth century, and was entirely the creation of one company's ad agency.

It's sobering to consider how many young men could otherwise have been spared so much grief and expense. But there are signs that that is changing.

Why diamonds?

In the 1860s, South African diamond mines owned by the De Beers cartel began producing over one million carats of diamonds a year. The market was flooded, prices came down, then in the 1920s firms like Cartier became household names with lavish diamond and precious stone rings (only for the rich, obviously).

With Art Deco (1920s–40s), diamonds went out of fashion with the younger generation who saw them as uninteresting and old fashioned, and this decline was sealed by the economic catastrophe of the Great Depression (1929–39) when prices collapsed.

The disengagement of the young was bad news for De Beers (with their near-monopoly on diamond production) as these were the consumers of the future. So in 1939, with the world recovering from its economic disaster, the cartel began their now famous advertising campaign with a programme to 'educate' the public about the '4Cs' of diamonds – 'colour, clarity, cut and carat weight'.

In 1947 they invented the slogan 'a diamond is forever', cleverly bringing together the physical properties of the mineral with the idea of a strong permanent marriage. Further campaigns included lines like 'Isn't two months' salary a small price to pay for something that lasts forever?' These were so successful that, to this day, the public is persuaded that (a) an engagement ring is indispensable for any proposal of marriage, (b) a diamond is the only acceptable stone for that ring and (3) a man must spend a very large chunk of his annual salary on an engagement ring.

Current trends

At the time of writing (2015) diamond prices are falling again, and coloured gemstones are becoming more fashionable and sought after. Women want something different and unique, and are beginning to see the diamond solitaire as somewhat old fashioned, rather mirroring the Art Deco revolt of the 1920s and 30s.

In the USA there is a movement away from engagement rings with stones altogether in favour of a series of plain or decorated bands for both men and women marking significant stages in a relationship. This reflects existing traditions in other countries, like Brazil for example.

All of this simply underlines that an engagement ring is a very individual purchase. And in my view, the more it becomes a decision about personal preference and style rather than a follow-the-herd purchase, the better.

Conclusion

While rings have been used for millennia as significant symbols in human relationships, the engagement ring is a fairly recent phenomenon, and diamond engagement rings in particular wax and wane in fashion and desirability.

The twentieth century preoccupation with diamonds was almost exclusively the creation of marketing campaigns. In the twenty-first century fashions are changing again – diamonds are losing their pre-eminence and coloured stones are in favour. Women are rejecting standard mass produced models, seeking unique individuality as a statement of their own personality to distinguish themselves from the herd.

This means that men who wish to use a ring as a token of their proposal can no longer rely on the standard diamond model to create a ring she will love forever. They have to get more inventive, and that means there is a lot more to know and take into account when designing and choosing the ring for a surprise proposal.

CHAPTER 7

ARE DIAMONDS ALWAYS 'A GIRL'S BEST FRIEND'?

The line 'Diamonds are a girl's best friend' is from the song famously rendered by Marilyn Monroe in the 1953 film 'Gentlemen Prefer Blondes'. It became part of the language, but has lost some of its bite – the lyrics are more about why mid-twentieth century women felt the need to pursue men who had money than the desirability of diamonds themselves.

Thankfully things have moved on a bit since then for women. And increasingly people want to understand the reality behind the mythology of diamonds.

Summary

- More people are interested in where their diamonds come from, but there is no completely ethically sourced diamond. The issue is part of the wider complexity of development in the poorest countries in the world

- The Kimberley Process (KP) was established to address some specific issues in the diamond supply chain, but in reality it makes the situation worse

- Boycotting diamonds from poor countries will not feed the people with the fewest life chances for whom they are the only source of income

- Some organisations do good work on improving conditions, but there is also too much 'greenwash'

- Just because a diamond has a certificate, or is described as 'certificated', *does not* mean that it is ethically sourced

- The only way things will really change is when consumers exercise their considerable buying power to demand it.

Ethics and the diamond supply chain

The price of diamonds depends on restriction of supply and on confidence. Confidence is the reason the industry is slowly responding to the widespread adverse publicity, provoked initially by the 2006 film *Blood Diamond*.

This film did have an impact on world diamond prices as a result of concerns about the link between diamond production, processing and distribution, and child labour, forced labour, dangerous working conditions, human rights abuses, poor mining practices, environmental degradation and the funding of genocidal civil war in Africa. The industry's response to this was the 'Kimberley Process', more of which later.

If you want a diamond, there are some 'ethical' options, but it is a bit of a moral minefield, and you have to be very careful because everyone is 'ethical' these days.

What is an ethical diamond?

Now there's a good question. What *is* an ethical diamond? It would seem a pretty straightforward thing to specify what makes a diamond ethical or not, but, as in most things in life, the ethics of the diamond supply chain come in all shades of grey.

Unless we've had our heads in the sand for the past few years, we know there are such things as 'blood diamonds' and these are very bad. But most people think it has all pretty much been solved by well-intentioned activists and NGOs hectoring governments into signing up to the 'Kimberley Process' so that we are in no danger of sullying our lovely sparkly jewellery and romantic proposals of marriage with horrid unethical diamonds.

I do so wish that were true. I would love to be able to say to my clients 'Buy these diamonds – they are good' or 'Don't buy these diamonds, they are very bad', so why can't I?

Well, there *are* some more ethically produced diamonds with fewer questions over their production, manufacture and sale. Apart from diamonds grown in a laboratory, there are diamonds mined in Namibia, Botswana and other places which make very positive contributions to the welfare and economy of whole countries or communities. The trick is knowing where they come from.

Then there are Canadian diamonds, mined in the pristine North West Territories of Canada since the 1990s with Canadian-type attention to good labour practices, aboriginal sensitivities and minimising environmental impact, and then cut and polished in Canada (very important that last bit). Set in fair trade/fair mined precious metals, these could be considered the Gold Standard of ethically produced diamond jewellery.

Even then, there are still concerns about the treatment of aboriginal peoples and their lands, and these diamonds constitute a tiny fraction of the world's diamond production. They would never satisfy global demand, and there is still the small fact that the miners are digging up pristine wilderness to get them out. But there's more.

Even if overnight the Canadians could supply the whole world's demand for diamonds in this way, and everyone bought these diamonds without the price going through the roof, what would happen to the livelihoods of the poorest people in the world who depend on the production of other less-than-ethical diamonds for their daily cup of rice?

A certificate is not a guarantee of ethical sourcing

Many people mistakenly believe that if a diamond has a certificate of grading or quality, this guarantees that it is ethically sourced. This is not true. The confusion arises from a misunderstanding of the function of the certificate.

Diamond certification is covered in more detail in Chapter 8.

It's all about development

The issue of ethical diamonds is not just about diamond production, it is about development in the poorest countries of the world, and development issues are very complicated. They can't be solved overnight, and it will take decades of joining up international and governmental action before things improve markedly. But this does not mean that we don't all have personal choices to make.

If we care about environmental degradation, human rights, hunger and malnutrition, education and health in developing countries, we need to understand how our purchases will impact on the poorest people of the world. If we are to make informed choices about our own personal footprint, we need to educate ourselves about these issues.

The ideal cut?

It's not just about where the diamonds come from or how they are mined, what about where they are cut and polished?

Around 82% of the world's diamonds are cut and polished in the city of Surat in India. Most people think it's done in places like Amsterdam, but since ancient times India has been a centre for diamonds. The first diamonds were mined there more than 1,000 years BC, and Alexander the Great brought the first diamond to Europe from India in 327 BC. For almost two thousand years, until the end of the nineteenth century, India was the only country in the world where diamonds were mined. Naturally, diamond cutting also originated in India, and diamonds have been skilfully cut and polished by Indian craftsmen since the beginning of the sixteenth century. It is a major centre of diamond production.

So the craftsmanship is certainly not in question, but the working and employment conditions of many of the people involved in the trade in India do not bear scrutiny. There are some honourable exceptions and concerted efforts to improve standards generally, but unless you know *where* and *how* the stones were cut, this cannot as yet be guaranteed as there is no method of tracking individual diamonds from mine to market.

The Kimberley Process Certification Scheme

I mentioned the Kimberley Process. If you have read anything at all on the ethics of diamonds, I expect you thought that these problems had all been sorted out by this international certification scheme.

It started as a genuine attempt to tackle some of the worst problems associated with the diamond industry, but it has such serious flaws that it may even make the situation worse. Global Witness, the NGO which was instrumental in establishing the Kimberley Process, withdrew in 2011, calling the whole organisation 'an accomplice to diamond laundering'.

What is the Kimberley Process? The Kimberley Process Certification Scheme (KP for short) was launched in 2003.

It is an international diamond certification system, focusing exclusively on stopping the trade in 'conflict diamonds'. These are defined by the KP as *'rough* diamonds used by *rebel* movements or their allies to finance armed conflicts aimed at undermining *legitimate governments'* – my italics. You can already see that all those qualifying words limit its scope drastically. Eighty countries participate in the KP, representing most of the nations involved in the diamond trade. The diamond industry, NGOs and advocate organisations concerned with human rights and the environment are also represented.

Member countries agree not to produce conflict diamonds, to trade diamonds only with each other and to attach KP certificates to their exports of rough uncut diamonds. The purpose is to keep conflict diamonds out of the certified diamond supply. *But* it is easily evaded by diamond smugglers, and worse, it is so limited in scope that it grants 'conflict free' certification to diamonds mined in violent and inhumane settings.

What Global Witness says about the Kimberley Process

Global Witness (www.globalwitness.org) first exposed the problem of blood diamonds in 1998 and played a key role in establishing the Kimberley Process (KP), a government-led certification scheme initiated in a bid to clean up the diamond trade. The scheme was launched in 2003 and requires member states to set up an import and export control system for rough diamonds. Over seventy-five of the world's diamond producing, trading and manufacturing countries participate in the scheme.

Conflict diamonds are defined by the Kimberley Process as 'rough diamonds used by rebel movements to finance wars against legitimate governments'. As a result of this narrow definition, the Kimberley Process is not empowered to address the broader range of risks to human rights posed by the trade in diamonds, such as those which have been documented in Zimbabwe.

It has persistently refused to broaden this definition, despite pressure from a range of civil society organisations. It has also faced persistent enforcement issues throughout its short history, the situation in Central African Republic (CAR) being the latest example – despite it placing an embargo on diamonds sourced from CAR in 2013, conflict diamonds sourced from areas under the control of armed groups in the country still reached international markets.

The Kimberley Process applies only to rough diamonds. Once stones are cut and polished, they are no longer covered by the scheme. The diamond trade undertook to deliver a meaningful and independently verifiable system of warranties, but has yet to deliver on that commitment. Ultimately, loopholes in the Kimberley Process and the failure to adapt to address a broader range of human rights concerns effectively means that diamonds associated with abuses are still contaminating global markets.

Persistent and unresolved concerns over these issues led Global Witness to resign as an official observer of the Kimberley Process in 2011. The past decade has proven that the Kimberley Process cannot clean up the diamond sector on its own.

Global Witness is calling on diamond companies, and the diamond industry as a whole, to play its role in breaking links with human rights abuses by conducting supply chain checks known as human rights due diligence.

For more information see: www.globalwitness.org/campaigns/conflict-diamonds

The Kimberley Process does not guarantee ethical diamonds. The Kimberley Process does very little to stop violence, worker exploitation and environmental degradation tied to diamond mining. These are the most pressing ethical problems facing the diamond industry today. Its definition for certification is very narrow. If a diamond has not funded the *rebel* side of a civil war, it is not considered a conflict diamond. This means that a diamond receiving KP certification may still be tied to killings, beatings, rape, and torture by a government army. It may have been mined using child labour, or by adults earning a dollar a day, and it may have destroyed the local environment where it was mined.

By certifying unethically mined diamonds, the KP provides legitimacy to human rights abusers. It misleads consumers into believing that their diamonds come from certified ethical sources when many diamonds approved by the process cause untold human suffering.

Nor does the KP certify individual diamonds or require them to be traceable to their mine of origin. It is applied to a batch of rough diamonds which are then cut and shipped around the world. Without a tracking system, this is where the trail ends, making it easy to smuggle banned diamonds into the certified supply. On top of this there is no real regulation of the diamond supply chain as it does not require the independent audit of buyers and sellers, permitting diamonds of unsavoury origin to enter the chain at any point.

The failure to impose controls has left the door wide open to diamond smuggling, making it even harder to prevent banned diamonds from entering the diamond supply. It also makes diamonds a favourite international currency for criminals, money launderers, tax evaders, drug dealers, and even terrorist groups such as Al Qaeda.

To add further injury to insult, as smugglers don't pay taxes, the governments of these mostly developing countries are deprived of much needed funds for basic services. In some cases, as in Zimbabwe, government officials themselves trade in smuggled diamonds, stealing hundreds of millions of dollars from the Zimbabwean treasury. Even the United States Government Accountability Office (GAO), an investigative arm of the US Government, has determined that diamond smuggling into the US is a serious problem.

So much for the international Kimberley Process Certification Scheme. But that is what people rely on when they say that a diamond is 'conflict free'. Most people assume that means ethically sourced. It does not.

So should you boycott all diamonds?

If only it were that simple. The issues and challenges surrounding the diamond industry are fundamentally the problems of development in the poorest parts of the world. And the answers to these problems are never simple or clear cut.

Development issues are very complicated. Sometimes, the most well intentioned interventions, taken without full knowledge and understanding of these complexities, make life much worse for the very people they were intended to help. I know that well from my time as an overseas aid worker in South America.

Take a topic as seemingly straightforward as food aid. People don't have enough food, we have too much. Give our surplus food to the people who need it more. Job done. Simple, no?

No. This is how complicated it can be: unless the food aid is being given to relieve an immediate crisis in the food supply, such as famine, flood, war, etc., and is properly administered and controlled, the routine 'dumping' of excess food in developing countries can completely destroy the local agricultural economy. It can put native farmers out of business by undermining their markets and reducing their prices. It can even lead to a criminal black market trade in 'aid food' and drive the farmers to grow illegal drug crops because they can no longer survive on the reduced income from food crops. Ultimately the consequences could be that a community becomes even less self-reliant in food, more dependent on aid, and the whole local agricultural economy becomes controlled by criminal groups. A truly vicious spiral of decline. The road to hell is paved with good intentions.

If food aid is that complex, industrial development in these countries is at least equally so.

The fact is that however appalling and unacceptable the conditions of mineworkers or the ecological degradation of the mining process, some of the poorest people in the world depend on the diamond industry for the bare minimum of survival. They have no alternative, or their alternatives are likely to be worse. But buying these diamonds also perpetuates the existing supply conditions. The only solution would be for their governments to provide or facilitate more alternatives. This is beginning to happen, but there is a lot more to do.

Kimberley, Zimbabwe and Sierra Leone

Martin Rapaport is a leading diamond industry figure and was a principal in setting up the Kimberley Process. He resigned in 2009 after the scheme authorised exports from two companies operating in the Marange diamond fields in Zimbabwe. In 2008 the Zimbabwean army seized control of the area, and in doing so reportedly killed about 200 miners, prompting Martin to say that 'Instead of eliminating blood diamonds, the KP has become a process for the systematic legalisation and legitimisation of blood diamonds'.

In a 2013 video, he outlined in graphic detail the stark choices people dependent on diamond mining can face. He gave the example of one fifteen-year-old boy, orphaned by AIDS and panning for diamonds in Sierrra Leone, who supports his thirteen-year-old sister with a cup of rice a day. Unacceptable yes, but until there is a coordinated response to the problem which includes education, agriculture and alternative employment options, what choices do he and his sister have?

To view Martin's video see:
https://www.youtube.com/watch?v=ubev11L6B_8

Conclusion – What is the answer?

As well as Canada, there are a number of countries where diamond mining benefits the whole population, as in Namibia and Botswana. Australia also produces a large proportion of the world's diamonds, but again there are environmental and aboriginal issues to be addressed.

At the moment, there is no right answer. Ideally what is needed is a system for certifying fair trade diamonds. Most people think that is what the Kimberley Process does, but as we have seen this is far from the case.

There are important initiatives towards achieving improvements in the sector from organisations like the Diamond Development Initiative International (DDII), the Alliance for Responsible Mining (ARM) and the RJC (Responsible Jewellery Council), but we are not there yet.

And there is a danger that some of this is just 'greenwash' designed to make the sector look better without really changing anything.

Nevertheless, it is important for consumers to be aware of the issues and ask the right questions of their jeweller. Pressure from informed consumers is the only way that real change will happen. No bride wants blood on her hands, and you have power as a consumer to change the world for the better through the choices you make.

CHAPTER 8

ALL YOU *NEED* TO KNOW ABOUT DIAMONDS

Diamonds are *not* the only stone for an engagement ring. They are not even a 'traditional' stone for the ring, but if you've done any research at all online, you'll have found that there's an awful lot written about them. Much of what is written is intended to 'romance the 'stone' – create a story around the subject, getting you to buy into the 'subtle complexity' of the diamond and pay more for the privilege.

If you are still keen to have a diamond in your engagement ring, the following chapter covers pretty much all you will need to know. Applying that information to any individual diamond might require a bit more expertise.

Summary

- Diamond grading is an art, not a science. There is no such thing as an accurate description of a diamond, other than its weight and physical dimensions

- Decide on your own priorities. Key criteria are: size, colour, quality, cost, origin and certification

- Size is measured in carats (weight) as well as mm (dimensions). Sometimes the latter is more useful

- Colour is graded on different scales. For most people there is little visible difference between the top six GIA colour grades

- Fluorescence is irrelevant except in very special circumstances

- Quality includes things like cut and clarity, both of which are subjective assessments.

A little information is a dangerous thing

You may have read a lot about the '4Cs' of diamonds – shorthand for colour, clarity, cut and carat. These are the supposed key criteria for judging a stone, and you might think that all you have to do is get the right certificate with the right letters on it and job done!

The concept of the 4Cs was originally devised by the GIA (Gemmological Institute of America) in part to provide some certainty to consumers and a recognised standard by which diamonds could be assessed. But it quickly became yet another marketing device promoted by the jewellery industry to segment the market and create the illusion that diamonds are somehow different from any other gemstone. As a means of describing a diamond, the 4Cs concept is useful up to a point – for example, to establish some minimum criteria. But given the variability of the standards applied by different laboratories, each description requires so many caveats that it can be more confusing than enlightening. Some diamond merchants even issue disclaimers with all certified stones, GIA or otherwise, to the effect that they do not offer any warranty or guarantee of the accuracy of the description in the certificate.

Diamond grading is an art, not a science. Apart from carat weight, which can be objectively measured, grading the remaining Cs – colour, cut and clarity – depends on the stringency of the criteria of the individual laboratories and certification bodies, and ultimately on the human being doing the grading. Whether any one diamond is a colour F or K, for example, may largely be a matter of opinion, and there is a wide variation in standards.

So be aware that, taken at face value, some of the 'information' available to you could be a touch misleading.

The strictly technical data is accurate (i.e. what can be objectively measured), but there is a strong tendency to try to persuade you that only certain colour grades and features are acceptable. Naturally these are the more expensive, and what constitutes the 'best quality' is a moveable feast.

Priorities

The most important thing is for you to decide on your priorities. When you know what you want to get from your purchase, and why, you are less likely to be led into spending more than you need to achieve your goals.

You know what your overall budget is, and if diamond is your main stone, this will probably take up the largest part of that. So you want to aim for the best balance between your priorities within your budget. You may decide that diamond size is the most important element, and you may be prepared to compromise on the colour, clarity or cut, or a combination of all three. You can always find a diamond for your budget or fit your budget to the diamond, it is up to you.

Apart from cost, the key considerations are:

- Size – it usually matters here

- Colour – generally white rather than yellow, unless you are setting directly into yellow or rose gold or want a fancy coloured stone

- Quality – it should sparkle and not have any visible black bits (carbon inclusions)

- Origin and provenance – something you may not yet have considered

- Certification – there are a number of certification bodies to choose from, but not all apply the same standards.

Not as catchy as the 4Cs perhaps, but a more practical way to look at the problem.

Size: carats

The size of a diamond is described by its weight in carats (ct–UK, or kt–USA).

Do not compare the prices of a 1.0ct solitaire to a 1.0ct trilogy ring with three smaller diamonds. A single diamond of 1.0ct costs much more than three stones whose weights add up to 1.0tcw. This is because larger diamond crystals are less common than smaller ones so command a higher price *per carat.*

If a ring has more than one diamond, it will be described using its total carat weight. This *should* be expressed as 'tcw' or 'ct (tw)', but is often displayed just as 'ct', which can be confusing because it may lead you to believe that the main stone is a higher carat than it is. For example, some retailers will describe a ring as 1.0ct when it contains a 0.5ct central diamond together with twenty-five diamonds of 0.02ct each in the halo and shank. To avoid confusing the consumer, the correct way to describe such a ring would be 1.0tcw because the total value of the diamonds is much less than a single 1.0ct stone.

An Explanations of 'Carats' (cts)

There are about five carats in a gramme, so 1ct = 0.20g

Carats are divided into 'points', so 1ct = 100 points

A half-carat diamond can be described as '50 points', and '10 points' is 0.01ct or 0.002g. The weights are tiny (and originally based on the weight of a carob seed, hence the name).

A 1.0ct diamond can cost ten times as much as a 0.33ct (otherwise of the same specification) for just three times the weight. In the example above, the 1.0ct trilogy ring might be half the price of the 1.0ct solitaire*.

*Assuming the same mount costs and based on prices for GIA certified FSI1 excellent-cut round brilliants at the time of writing.

Size: dimensions

If size is an issue, and it often is when we are talking diamonds, it may be more useful for your purposes to know the dimensions of a stone. There is a standard for the relationship between the carat weight and dimensions of any shape of diamond. This is based on the 'ideal cut' for that shape.

But stones are cut to maximise their value, which, more often than not, means their carat weight. So any reasonable quality of diamond is available in a wide range of dimensions. The quality of the cut is directly related to how much sparkle you will see in a stone. Both a very flat cut and a very deep cut diamond will lose brilliance so the ratio is important, but may be less noticeable than the impact of the size of the stone on the hand. Yet another reason why you do need to establish your priorities and why expert guidance will ensure you get the best value for your purchase.

Comparing sizes

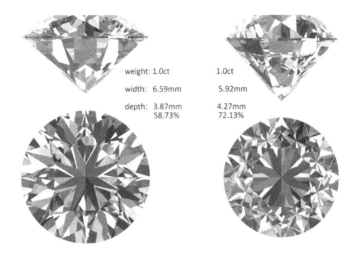

weight:	1.0ct	1.0ct
width:	6.59mm	5.92mm
depth:	3.87mm	4.27mm
	58.73%	72.13%

Comparison of the relative sizes of two actual GIA certified round brilliant 1.0ct diamonds

Comparison of table sizes of two 1.0ct round diamonds

Diameter 1 5.92mm (Depth 1 4.27mm; ratio – 72.1%)

Diameter 2 6.59mm (Depth 2 3.87mm; ratio – 58.8%)

So, diamond #2 is 0.67mm (11%) wider than diamond #1. This may not seem much, but the difference is visible. To put it into perspective: a standard 0.75ct brilliant is about 0.7mm wider than a 0.5ct, and a standard 1.5ct is about 1.0mm wider than a 1.0ct.

Colour

After the size of the diamond, the colour is usually the next most important consideration, and this is where opinion starts to come into the equation. When comparing data on graded diamonds, be aware that the opinion of one certification body may differ from that of another for the same stone.

Each diamond certification body sets its own standards, and any qualified diamond grader will use his or her judgement within the acceptable ranges permitted by the certification body. Many ready-made engagement rings do not come with an independent grading certificate, so the opinion on colour (and quality) is that of the seller. There is clearly an even greater potential for variation here.

Diamond colour is graded from D, the whitest of diamonds, down through the letters of the alphabet to fancy yellows and brown diamonds, all the way to black. For most practical purposes, diamonds are still considered 'white' in the range D to J. These are most suitable for rings set in platinum or white gold.

If your ring is to be yellow or rose gold, it is worth thinking about a colour K to M as these warmer tints sit well in gold and are much less costly than whiter stones. In fact, a K diamond is often half the price of an otherwise similar

G diamond – *as long as they have been certified by the same laboratory.*

There is a fine distinction between each of the colours. Most people cannot detect differences between one colour and the next, and for a single diamond the distinction is even less obvious. Ice white is not everyone's cup of tea, and there is a subtle beauty in the very faintly yellow tints. It is all down to personal preference, and unless you can compare two stones directly it is pretty difficult for the lay person to tell whether they are looking at a colour D or G anyway.

Fancy coloured diamonds. Almost all diamonds fall within the standard D to Z colour classification, but there are what are called 'fancy coloured diamonds' in blues, pinks, deep yellows and even green. Some coloured diamonds are treated as naturally occurring fancy coloured diamonds are very rare, much prized and a lot more costly. One of the best known mines for fancy pink diamonds is the Argyle Mine in Western Australia.

Colours can range from a subtle tint to strong, deep hues, and the deeper the colour, generally speaking, the more valuable the stone, if natural. In these stones, brilliance and fire are less of a consideration.

As with all diamonds, very small fancy stones are unlikely to come with their own grading certificate, but it is important to have a certificate for any coloured diamond over 0.25ct so that you can be sure of its provenance.

Fluorescence. The apparent colour of a white diamond can be influenced by 'fluorescence'. This is natural in about 25% of diamonds seen under ultra-violet light, including daylight. It is the same effect as seen in white clothes or teeth when you stand under a blue or ultraviolet light (which anyone who has ever been to a nightclub will recognise).

In diamonds, fluorescence is the result of ultra-violet radiation causing electrons to move within the diamond's crystal structure. So much for the science. There is no need to worry about fluorescence – in most cases there is no practical effect, and because the most common type is blue it will make yellowish diamonds look whiter, so improving their appearance.

If you are matching diamonds in a ring or pair of earrings and fluorescence is present, it is as well to make sure that the stones are broadly similar, otherwise they won't match under UV light.

The good news is that fluorescence can reduce the price of a diamond, as well as making a stone look a better colour than its grading might suggest. Win-win, I think.

Quality: clarity and cut

Clarity. Clarity refers to the number, type and visibility of inclusions (bits of material and crystalline faults) in the stone. It determines how 'sparkly' any cut of diamond can be, as the higher the level of clarity, the fewer inclusions there are to get in the way of light passing through the stone.

As with all things diamond-related, it all depends what sort of inclusion, how big it is, whether it is faint and white or a black speck of carbon, and where it appears on the stone. Does the way the stone is cut help to reduce the appearance of the inclusion? For example, the inclusions in a 1.0ct emerald cut diamond are more apparent than the same inclusions in a round brilliant because the latter has more facets and throws light around in more directions, so obscuring minor inclusions.

How Clarity is described (GIA)

Clarity is graded by the GIA as follows:

- IF – Internally Flawless, which speaks for itself

- VVS 1 & 2 – Very, very slightly included. Inclusions can't be seen with the naked eye and are very difficult to see even under 10x magnification

- VS1 & 2 – Very slightly included. Again, inclusions are not visible to the naked eye, but may be visible under 10x magnification

- SI1 & 2 – Slightly included. Inclusions are visible under 10x magnification and, rarely, to the unaided eye

- I1 & 2 – Included. You can see these inclusions with the naked eye. Sometimes this requires close inspection, and the smaller the diamond or the more facets it has, the less important that might be.

Cut. There are two aspects to cut – quality and type. The quality element of cut is highly complex, subjective and the most difficult for a non-specialist to assess.

The quality of cut is generally graded from excellent, through good to poor. The cut may also be described as ideal, shallow or deep. These describe the ratio of surface to depth.

A shallow cut will give you more surface area (i.e. the stone appears bigger) for a given carat weight, and a deep cut the reverse. As you can see from the image, the depth of the cut will also affect the apparent brilliance of the stone as light is reflected at a different angle. A 'poor' cut can spoil a stone, and an 'excellent' one can elevate it.

Most diamonds are cut to maximise carat weight and brilliance, so there is always a compromise between these elements, and the diamond will be priced accordingly.

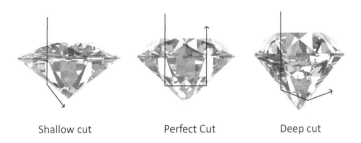

Shallow cut   Perfect Cut   Deep cut

**How light is deflected in ideal, shallow
and deep cut brilliants**

The type of cut does make a difference to the sparkle factor as it determines the number of facets you can expect in a stone. Modern cuts, like the 'brilliant' cut, are designed to create the maximum sparkle for the stone. All other things being equal, the more facets you have, the more sparkly a diamond will be. New designs for cuts do come to the market from time to time, and these are usually trademarked.

Older pieces of jewellery sometimes have diamonds with antique styles of cut, like the 'rose' cut. These are more subtle and don't have the brilliance of modern stones, so if you are using inherited stones and need to find a match to add to the design, this will require some care.

Certification

Diamond certification is often referred to as the 'fifth C'. So what is it? And why is it important?

A diamond certificate is intended to provide third party information about the characteristics of a diamond, including grading its colour, clarity, cut and the carat weight. It is supposed to help you understand what you are buying and will tell you if a diamond has been treated to enhance it in any way, as this would affect its market value and price. There are also specific certificates for laboratory created diamonds.

I want to correct one common misunderstanding about diamond certificates and it is this: *a diamond certificate is **not** a guarantee that a diamond has been mined in an ethical or ecologically sustainable manner.* Certification is only about the physical characteristics of the stone, not its sourcing or the supply chain.

The GIA was the first to introduce what has become the best known and most trusted system of diamond grading and certification. The importance of a certificate for a diamond lies in the extent to which it offers you assurance that you are getting what you pay for. The danger in buying an uncertified diamond, or one which has been certified by the seller, is simply that without a certificate the seller can represent the diamond as being whatever he wishes it to be, and will charge accordingly.

You also have to ask yourself (and the retailer) why a diamond is not certified. Certified diamonds carry more value in the market than uncertified diamonds, so there would have to be a very good reason why a retailer had not had the diamond certified. Do not be put off by the claims that 'it takes too long' or 'it's too expensive to get a certificate'. The extra cost of certification is outweighed by the additional value having it confers.

You will also find that diamonds certified by different bodies have different prices. This is because the market discounts up to a point the differences in grading standards in the price which a stone can command. But if you don't know which laboratories are the most lax, or can't evaluate the diamond yourself, you could pay more than you should.

Do be aware that round diamonds smaller than 0.3ct are rarely certified because they are too small to warrant the cost of certification. For other shapes, such as oval and square, the minimum weight for certification can be higher, and very small diamonds, known as 'mêlée', are never certified. For anything else, get one with a certificate.

The salutary tale of the 'DVS1' diamond

A couple came to me for wedding rings by recommendation from one of their friends. At the same time they asked for my opinion on the engagement ring which they had bought only six months before in a shop in London's jewellery quarter, Hatton Garden.

Not knowing where best to start when buying their ring, like many people they thought this would be *the* place to find it. They found a design they liked and were sold the ring as a 0.7ct DVS1 diamond at a price they thought was a very good deal. But there was no independent certificate to verify the grading of the diamond.

Even by eye it was clear to me that the diamond they thought was a colour D was actually nearer H or I. That is four or five grades of colour lower than they believed they had purchased! But because there was no independent certificate (and colour grading is then a matter of personal opinion), there was little they could do to remedy the situation.

While the price they paid *would* have been a good deal if the diamond were a GIA certified D colour, they had paid more than they should have done for a stone whose correct grade was H or I. Given the gross overstatement of the colour, it was not surprising to discover that the retailer had also graded clarity with equal laxity. So they lost out on both counts.

This story just underlines the need to be absolutely sure about the reliability of anyone from whom you buy an uncertified diamond. Why would a 0.7ct DVS1 diamond not be certified? If you are not sure, specify that the purchase is subject to testing and arrange for the stone to be independently certified by a reputable laboratory *of your choice*. If you can do this *before* you buy, even better. It will be worth the relatively small investment in the laboratory fees.

A caveat about certificates

There is an argument that retailers, especially online, concentrate too much on the certificate and not enough on the diamond itself. This reflects the fact that, although certificates are intended to provide some certainty to the buyer, because diamond grading is so subjective, they are only a guide. Even with GIA certificates, you could line up four diamonds with the same certificated colour grading and they would be four different colours.

Recently, there has been a lot of concern within the industry about deliberate over-grading on diamond certificates. Grading largely determines price, so in some cases this practice is fraud and there have been arrests by US authorities. This fraud can be perpetrated precisely because so much reliance and confidence is placed in the certificate, particularly when diamonds are sold online.

A Note on Certifying Organisations

There are a number of organisations which certify diamonds, the most well-known being the GIA (Gemmological Institute of America). The GIA is also the leading independent grading laboratory with offices around the world. It offers educational services and is the longest established of the grading organisations. Over time it has pretty much set the standards for diamond grading and established the concept of the 4Cs.

In the USA, the AGSL (American Gemmological Society Laboratories) is especially known for its in-depth scientific analysis of the technicalities of cut which are so important to diamond brilliance. AGSL uses a different scale to describe diamonds, but this can be compared directly with the more well-known GIA scale. Its standards on colour and clarity are directly comparable to GIA (AGSL uses a GIA graded master set of diamonds for colour grading), and its analysis of cut and light performance is better.

You will also come across IGI, HRD, and EGL, although there are others (see glossary for the full titles of these organisations). There is some dispute about the relative laxity of grading of the different laboratories, although GIA and AGSL are generally considered the strictest. As discussed earlier, there is always room for human opinion in the colour and clarity grading of diamonds. And there are so many potential variables it is difficult to conduct a definitive 'test' to identify which laboratories are stricter than others in all cases. Even within the same laboratory it is accepted that the same stone may be graded up or down by one grade of colour or clarity, depending on when or by whom it is graded, and this includes GIA and AGSL. Nevertheless, some jewellers will avoid certain of the grading laboratories.

Conclusion

Diamonds are a subject to which too much attention is paid and about which too much is written. My apologies for adding to that mountain of text.

Most of what is written is designed to make you believe that diamonds are special and create mystique around them.

There is no such thing as an accurate description of a diamond, other than its weight and physical dimensions. The truth is that unless you are trained or experienced in the subject of diamonds, you cannot know how accurate the description is on the certificate. That being said, you should ask why a diamond does not have a certificate as the fact of having one adds more to the price than the cost of obtaining one.

My only advice when it comes to buying diamonds, or any other gemstone, is treat online sellers with caution. If you want to be sure you are getting what you need *and* what you are paying for, consult a jeweller you know you can trust, and one you can look in the eye!

CHAPTER 9

ALL YOU NEED TO KNOW ABOUT GEMSTONES

If you hadn't thought about it before, I hope – having got this far – that you'll agree with me that an engagement ring does not have to mean diamonds. There are alternatives.

Other than diamonds, the main precious gemstones are sapphire, ruby and emerald, but there is an infinite variety of colour and texture in these, and many other gemstones. This chapter aims to provide some of the information you need about the gemstones you may be thinking of using. But it can only scratch the surface.

Each stone merits a book of its own, and there are gem dealers who specialise in one type of gemstone such as emerald or sapphire, but many jewellers are not specialists in coloured stones, and there is a great deal more complexity in choosing the right coloured stone than there ever will be in choosing a diamond. In this area, you really do need specialist help, preferably from a jeweller who knows a good and experience gem dealer.

Summary

- There are many more beautiful and unusual alternatives to diamonds for your engagement ring, including various coloured sapphires, ruby and emerald

- Some gemstones are not suitable for an engagement ring which is to be worn every day for a lifetime as they are too soft and easily damaged

- Various treatments can be applied to gemstones to enhance them. Some treatments are not acceptable. All must be declared at the point of sale.

- There is no certification process for coloured stones, like diamonds there's no mine to market tracing or guarantees, and production is unregulated. It is a matter of knowing who you are buying from

- Coloured gemstones are a highly technical area. Consumers can influence the industry by the buying choices they make, so choose your supplier carefully.

Beautiful, precious and durable – making sure it lasts a lifetime

If your intended loves colour, you may want something more unusual than just diamond, or you may be thinking about incorporating her birthstone or other significant gems. If so, you need to be aware that many gemstones are too soft to use in an engagement ring which will be worn every day.

Mohs scale. The hardness of gemstones is measured on the Mohs scale. This is a logarithmic scale designed in 1812 by Friedrich Mohs, a German geologist, to describe the relative hardness of minerals. The hardest mineral on the scale is diamond at 10; ruby and sapphire (both forms of Corundum) come in at 9, while Emerald is 7.5.

Gemstones to avoid. It is inadvisable to choose a stone rated below 7 for your ring as it won't stand up to daily wear for a lifetime and will probably have to be replaced after a few years. So, for an engagement ring I would certainly advise you to avoid opal, moonstone, amber, turquoise and pearl. These scratch easily and their surfaces are too delicate to withstand everyday chemicals.

Amethyst, garnet, iolite and tourmaline at 7–7.5 will abrade in time. Morganite, though a pretty pink and currently popular, will also abrade quickly, and even at 7.5 I do not recommend it for an engagement ring. Other popular stones like peridot and tanzanite really are too soft at 6.5–7.

Even if a gem is rated at 7 or over, if it's brittle, like emerald, the setting for the stone should be designed to protect it from damage, for example by using a bezel setting rather than claws (see Chapter 13).

Durable gemstones. These are the most durable or sought after gemstones for an engagement ring with their Mohs scale rating.

Gemstone	Mineral family	Colour range	Hardness on Mohs scale
Sapphire	Corundum	blue, pink, yellow, colourless	9
Ruby	Corundum	Red	9
Topaz	Silicate	colourless, red, yellow, pink-orange, grey, brown	8
Aquamarine	Beryl	shades of pale to intense light blue	7.5–8
Spinel	Spinel	red, blue, green, yellow, brown, black	7.5-8
Emerald	Beryl	rich deep green	7.5

Here is a brief rundown on these beautiful colourful gems.

Sapphire

Blue Sapphire is a really popular choice for engagement rings and is one of the four precious gems. Like ruby, it is a form of corundum and therefore very hard and durable. Sapphire is an expensive stone, but it is worth getting the best quality you can afford because the lower grade, cheaper stones, which are commonly used, can be very dark in colour, verging on black, and have no fire or brilliance.

The colours of sapphire

Blue is the best known colour for sapphire, from a light true blue through to a deep indigo, the intensity depending on the amount of titanium and iron in the crystal. A medium coloured cornflower blue is the most desirable.

Sapphire does come in a range of other colours, including colourless, pale pink, orange, green, yellow, violet and brown – known as 'fancy sapphires'. Paparadscha sapphire, a peachy pink, is a particularly lovely and unusual shade which is becoming very popular, but be aware that a 'pink sapphire' is really a pale ruby. By definition rubies can only be red, so these stones are marketed as 'pink sapphire', which also sounds better than 'pale ruby'.

While sapphires are mined mainly in Australia, they are found in Sri Lanka, Thailand, China, Tanzania and Kenya. The best cornflower blue is very rare indeed and comes from Kashmir.

The name 'sapphire' is from 'sapphirus', Latin for blue, and the Greek 'sappheiros' from the island off the Arabian Sea where sapphires were first found. During the Middle Ages, priests wore sapphires as protection from impure thoughts and warriors gave their young wives sapphire necklaces to ensure fidelity. Sapphire is September's birthstone and is also given on fifth and forty-fifth wedding anniversaries.

Ruby

Ruby is another popular gemstone for engagement rings. It is one of the four precious gems and, as one of the most valued gemstones throughout history, it has an extensive mythology. Like sapphire, it is a form of corundum, so is hard and durable.

Ruby

The red colour is created by traces of chromium in the crystal, and only red corundum can be called ruby. The range of reds varies with the individual deposits and locations, the most desirable colour, called 'pigeon's blood', being a pure red with a hint of blue. As a rough stone, ruby appears dull, but when cut, the lustre can be almost as good as diamond, and inclusions in rubies are common.

In recent years there has been a supply problem because the best rubies come from Burma (Myanmar). The country has been the subject of International trade embargoes owing to its poor human rights record. At the time of writing, it is still not possible to buy Burmese rubies in the USA, so a lot of Burmese ruby is channelled through Thailand and is misleadingly sold as of Thai origin. This may change with the democratisation of Burma/Myanmar.

Rubies are also found in Sri Lanka, Cambodia, parts of Africa and the USA.

Ancient Hindus believed that the red of ruby came from an eternal flame that could not be put out, making the stone a symbol of everlasting love. Ruby is the birthstone for July and is also given to celebrate fifteen and forty years of marriage.

Emerald

Emerald belongs to the beryl family of gemstones and is one of the precious gemstones. Highly valued as a gemstone for at least 4,000 years, a rich deep green is the most desirable colour and is the result of traces of chromium and vanadium in the beryl. Owing to its structure it is brittle and relatively easily scratched, chipped and damaged. If it is to be worn as an engagement ring, the ring must be designed to protect the stone as much as possible and treated with great care. It will abrade and will need repolishing in time. But emerald *is* the rarest and most precious stone.

Emerald

Beryl, vanadium and chromium do not occur naturally in the same geographical areas. So emerald is only formed when violent geological events occur which bring these minerals together. Owing to its dramatic formation, emerald is more brittle than other beryls, so the famous 'emerald cut' was developed for this gemstone to alleviate the amount of pressure required during the cutting process.

Emeralds almost always contain inclusions and minute fractures or fissures, again as a result of their violent formation, so for thousands of years, emeralds have been treated with oils and resins to make the fissures less obvious and enhance the clarity of the stone. These fissures are called 'jardin', owing to their likeness to garden foliage.

The name for the stone comes from the Greek 'Smaragdos', via the Vulgar Latin variant 'Esmeraldus', meaning green stone. The earliest finds were near the Red Sea in Egypt, and it was a favourite of Cleopatra, who wore particularly lavish emerald jewellery. Hence the mines were dubbed 'Cleopatra's Mines' when they were rediscovered in the early nineteenth century. Now, the main emerald producing country is Colombia, but fine quality emeralds are also found in Brazil, parts of Africa, Pakistan, India, Afghanistan and Russia.

The ancient Romans dedicated the stone to Venus, the goddess of beauty and love, and associated emeralds with fertility and renewal. A gift of emerald is considered to be a sign of love and devotion. Emerald is the birthstone for May and given for twentieth and thirty-fifth wedding anniversaries.

Precious Topaz

Topaz has been used in jewellery for centuries but was elbowed out of fashion by the fad for diamonds. Pure Topaz is colourless and transparent, and was sometimes mistaken for diamond, although it does not have the same fire. The most famous topaz is a colourless stone of 1,680cts. Called the 'Braganza Diamond', it is set in the Portuguese Crown Jewels.

Precious Topaz

Golden yellow topaz is the most widely known precious topaz, and 'Imperial Topaz' can be yellow or, rarely, pink or pinky-orange. Topaz can also be clear. Be aware that many brown, grey or pale topazes are heat treated or irradiated to make them more saleable colours such as bright blue, yellow, gold, pink or even violet. Consequently, some topazes can fade if exposed to too much ultraviolet light.

Topaz is a hard gemstone found in many parts of the world, but like emerald it is brittle and should be worn with care.

'Topaz' is from the Greek 'Topazios', the name of an island in the Red Sea where yellow stones were mined, and in the Middle Ages 'topaz' was the name given to any yellow gemstone. Because of its colour, both the Egyptians and Romans believed that it was associated with the sun god, and Golden Topaz is the birthstone for November.

Aquamarine

Aquamarine is often used for engagement rings, perhaps partly because wearing an aquamarine is said to ensure a good marriage and bring the wearer happiness and good fortune.

Aquamarine

Aquamarine is the light blue variety of the mineral beryl, the same mineral as emerald. It is a beautifully clear stone with a wonderful shine and is almost completely free from inclusions, unlike emerald. It can range in colour from a very pale blue to a deep-sea blue, and even have a light green hue. The intensity of colour depends on the quantity of iron within the mineral, and the most valuable aquamarines are an intense blue. It is mostly mined in Brazil, but occurs in parts of Africa, Burma, Russia and Sri-Lanka.

The name comes from the Latin 'aqua' for water and 'mare' for sea. Since ancient times, aquamarine has been seen as a gemstone of vision, and aquamarine crystals were often used for eyes in Roman and Greek statues to symbolise power and wisdom.

Aquamarine is the birthstone for March and October, and is the nineteenth wedding anniversary stone.

Spinel

Spinel comes in a very wide range of colours, including red, blue, green and yellow. Although very beautiful, it is not now a commonly known gemstone. Both ruby and spinel are aluminium oxides, often found together, and before minerals were properly chemically classified, red spinel was equally known as ruby. So some of the most famous historical 'rubies' are in fact spinels, including the 'Black Prince's Ruby' and the 'Timur Ruby' in the British Crown Jewels.

Spinel

The largest known spinel in the world is the 500ct Samerian Spinel, once owned by a seventeenth century Indian Mughal emperor, and now part of the Iranian Crown Jewels. It is even believed to have once adorned the neck of the biblical golden calf, said to have been destroyed by Moses.

Spinel is certainly hard enough to be considered for use in an engagement ring, and its colour range would make it an unusual and individual choice.

Treatments to enhance diamonds and gemstones

There are a number of treatments which are routinely applied to both diamonds and gemstones to enhance their appearance, change their colours, stabilise, or otherwise improve the gem. Treatments include oiling, heating, dyeing, diffusion, irradiation, modifying inclusions in diamonds with the use of lasers as well as filling gems and diamonds with glass or resin.

Some treatments, such as filling with resin in order to deceive the customer, are not acceptable. Others have their benefits and are acceptable insofar as they are fully disclosed to the purchaser and the gem is priced accordingly. Some gemstones would hardly exist at all if it were not for common treatments, especially heat treating. An example is citrine, which is a heat treated amethyst. This occurs seldom in nature, so if it were not for heat treatment, those that were available would be much more expensive.

Any treatment which changes the colour or fundamental character of the stone will naturally affect its value and price. Some treatments are more acceptable than others and some are more obvious. Some are not permanent so the stone may degrade over time. Other treatments can make the stone less robust and so more liable to get damaged when it is worn. Unscrupulous dealers will attempt to sell treated diamonds and gemstones as natural.

All reputable stone dealers and jewellers will fully disclose relevant information about any stones they sell. This is why you must always buy your gemstones and diamonds from a reputable and knowledgeable source. Do be aware that there is no standard certification process for coloured gems as there is for diamonds, so you are reliant on the integrity of the person from whom you buy your gem.

Here's a brief review of some of the more common treatments. A full discussion would require a book of its own, so it's best to take expert advice.

Heat treatment. This is the most common treatment and is routinely applied to aquamarine, ruby, sapphire, tanzanite and zircon (both blue and colourless). Heating is only detectable by experts using special equipment and is usually irreversible under normal conditions.

It can lighten, darken, or completely change the colour of a stone, as well as improving clarity and brightness. Unheated rubies and sapphires will contain microscopic inclusions that show the stones have not been heated, but high quality unheated stones carry a very large price premium owing to their extreme rarity. Heat treatment brings beautiful gemstones within the reach of mere mortals.

Oiling. Oil is routinely applied to emerald, and sometimes to ruby and other stones, to fill surface fractures.

As mentioned earlier, the minerals which go to make up emerald do not occur naturally together in the Earth's crust, so emerald formation is the result of a confluence of cataclysmic forces. As a consequence, emeralds commonly contain many inclusions, fissures and minute cracks. These can make the individual emerald fragile and give it an uneven surface even when polished. To stabilise the stone, the majority of emeralds are oiled. As it is now a standard treatment for emerald, this is not generally disclosed as it is assumed that all cut, polished and finished mined stones will be oiled. Cultured or laboratory grown emeralds (see Chapter 10) do not require oiling.

Glass fill. The objective of glass fill is to improve the appearance of the gem by filling up all the gaps and fissures with coloured glass. It is a common procedure with lower grade ruby and must always be disclosed as it makes the ruby appear better quality than it actually is.

Irradiation. In order to improve their colour, some gemstones are irradiated. This treatment is often not permanent and must be disclosed as the gem can fade or change colour again, especially when exposed for long periods to ultraviolet light.

Blue topaz is irradiated either to make the blue stronger or to change lower grade brown or dirty yellow topaz into desirable blue. Many coloured diamonds are either heat treated or irradiated in order to change the colour of the oxides they contain. So certification is important if you want to make sure you have a natural pink, for example.

Lasers. Most diamonds contain inclusions of one sort or another, which are more or less visible to the naked eye. As diamonds are composed of carbon it is not surprising that the most obvious inclusions in diamonds will be little black specks of carbon. These can spoil an otherwise perfectly good stone. One way to reduce the appearance of these black inclusions is to drill tiny holes in the diamond and target them very precisely with lasers. The lasers 'burn' the carbon and turn a black spec into a much less visible feather or other artefact in the stone. This is a permanent treatment and can effectively improve the quality grading of a diamond, and therefore the treatment has an impact on its price. As with any treatment, laser treatment should be disclosed in the diamond's grading certificate.

Conclusion – sourcing gemstones

This brief discussion is designed to arm you with some useful information about coloured gemstones so that you can ask the necessary questions when deciding on the stone for your ring.

While the sourcing of coloured stones has not come under the same scrutiny as diamonds for ethical practices and ecological impact, there are many issues to address as production in most countries is completely unregulated. This does not mean it is all bad as there are both small scale and family-owned 'artisan' mines which are properly run, as well as larger well-run commercial enterprises. But, like the diamond supply chain, there is no tracking from mine to market, and for gemstones there is as yet no certification process, unlike diamonds.

A wide range of treatments is available for enhancing gemstones and diamonds. Most of these are entirely legitimate and accepted as long as they are declared at the point of purchase. The layperson is unlikely to be able to discern them.

The current danger is a concentration of ownership such as De Beers had over diamond production. This is unlikely to be a good thing for the consumer or the economies of the countries where these stones are mined. Again, the individual consumer can influence this by the choices they make when purchasing their stone, and by using a jeweller who cares about where their gemstone comes from and how it came to market.

When it comes to sourcing gemstones and assessing their quality and provenance, you are completely reliant on your jeweller for good advice and guidance. So it is worth asking the right questions.

CHAPTER 10

CULTURED GEMSTONES – AN ETHICAL ALTERNATIVE

As I have already discussed at length, there are a lot of ethical issues surrounding the mining and the supply chain of diamonds, gemstones and the precious metals used in jewellery.

There is one alternative which people in general know very little about, largely because the jewellery industry tries very hard to keep it under wraps and dismiss or belittle it whenever it comes up for discussion. This is the scientific culturing of *real* diamonds and *real* gemstones in a laboratory. These stones are physically, chemically and optically identical to mined stones, impossible to tell apart from the best quality mined gems except with specialist equipment, and are less costly, in all ways. So, if the ethical issue doesn't do it for you, there are other factors which might.

Summary

- Cultured gemstones and diamonds are *real* stones, have been around for a very long time, and can only be distinguished with high tech equipment

- The advantages are high quality, lower price ethical production and supply, as well as ready availability

- The jewellery trade has discouraged their use and this has created consumer prejudice

- They are not to be confused with simulants and imitations

- Buy only from a source you know provides the highest quality.

Cultured pearls

The best known cultured gems are cultured pearls. These are widely accepted and the best are quite costly, but culturing has made real pearls available to women all around the world who would otherwise have had to make do with glass and plastic imitations.

The process of creating cultured pearls was discovered by a British biologist in the early twentieth century and commercialised in Japan. The market for cultured pearls developed rapidly so that now 99% of pearls sold are cultured and grown in Japan and China.

Natural and cultured pearls can only really be distinguished by X-ray which can reveal the introduced nucleus. This is because cultured pearls are otherwise formed by exactly the same processes as wild pearls.

The large scale production of cultured pearls has removed the risk from the industry, reduced costs considerably and made high quality real pearl jewellery available to many more people.

A well-kept secret – cultured gemstones

I began with cultured pearls because of the many parallels with cultured gemstones and the fact that these pearls are universally accepted and known.

What is not so widely known is that cultured gemstones, grown in a laboratory over a period of three to twelve months or more, and similarly difficult to distinguish from the 'wild' variety, have been available since the 1930s. As well as addressing many of the ethical issues surrounding the gemstone supply chain, they also tackle some of the same issues of quality, cost and availability as did the introduction of cultured pearls. The mystery is why they have not taken off in the same way commercially.

I believe that this is largely the result of a real misunderstanding about the nature of cultured laboratory-grown gemstones, so, before you switch off, I want to emphasise that laboratory created diamonds and gemstones are *real* stones. They are not fake like cubic zirconium (Cz), glass and resin imitations. They are chemically, optically and physically identical to stones dug out of the ground. So much so that it is impossible for even an experienced gemmologist to tell the difference with certainty between these and high quality mined gemstones and diamonds without using very sophisticated equipment. In fact, specialist equipment has had to be created to detect more quickly the increasing numbers of laboratory grown diamonds finding their way into the supply chain illegally.

As good as the mined variety

Let me tell you a personal story of emeralds to illustrate the point. My husband wanted to give me a ring for our wedding anniversary, so we designed it together and I chose the stones. I love emeralds; what I don't like is not always being sure where and how they get to the ring on my finger. Large, good quality emeralds are also rare and very expensive, and like most people, my darling husband doesn't have bottomless pockets. So, for different reasons, we are both advocates of created emeralds, particularly those produced by Chatham Laboratories since the 1930s.

After many drafts, the ring was duly made in 18ct yellow gold and platinum with five Chatham emeralds and two Canadian diamonds. Having initially designed it to go with my wedding band, I decided that I wanted to wear it on its own on my right hand. Right is bigger than left, so I took it to be resized. When I dropped by my repairs workshop to collect it, the resident gemmologist came over and congratulated me, commenting that I had 'some lovely emeralds in that ring'. He had been examining it for quality assurance of their work and was struck, he said, by their excellent colour and grade, and that they looked very much like the best Colombian stones. I thanked him and said that I was really pleased to have found them, without saying where. I did not want to embarrass him by letting on that they were cultured emeralds, but I was very happy to know that even an expert using high magnification could not tell the difference.

Cultured gemstones vs the rest

One thing we need to get clear right from the start is the difference between created, or cultured, laboratory-grown gemstones (also known as synthetic) on one hand, and simulants and imitations on the other. The terms 'created', 'cultured', 'laboratory-grown' and 'synthetic' mean the same thing and are interchangeable. The term 'synthetic' is often misused and given a pejorative slant.

Simulants and imitations are *not* the same thing as mined stones, whereas cultured/synthetic stones are physically the same in every respect.

Cultured stones. As illustrated above, cultured gemstones, including diamonds, are chemically identical to mined stones. They are very difficult to tell from naturally occurring gems, and highly sophisticated equipment is needed to identify them.

There are a couple of different patented methods for creating gemstones and diamonds. Laboratory grown stones are specified as such with their own recognised classification, and synthetic diamonds have their own special GIA grading reports so that the consumer is fully aware of what they are buying.

Good quality emeralds, rubies and sapphires of a reasonable size are rare and expensive. Although growing them in a laboratory takes time, it doesn't take as long as growing them in the ground.

It is costly to produce synthetic gems and they take time to make, typically up to twelve months for larger stones depending on the method. So, although they offer a significantly less expensive alternative, they should not be thought of as 'cheap', because they are not.

Laboratory created gemstones are very pure and high quality. Synthetic rubies can look like the highest grade naturally occurring stones, and the same can be said of synthetic diamonds. As is so often the case, their greatest strength can also be a weakness, depending on what you want from your gems. Their chemical purity means that there are no natural inclusions in the stones. This is a good thing because they then have greater brilliance. The colours are clear and bright, and cultured sapphires are a particularly lovely shade of cornflower blue.

Nevertheless, some people want the variation and character which inclusions can bring to gemstones, in spite of their negative impact on clarity. This can be particularly so in the case of emeralds, where inclusions are common and are given the rather romantic name of 'jardin'. I suspect this to be a clear case of making a virtue of a necessity, and I'm happy to have a lovely large ethically produced emerald which I can afford.

Apart from the significant cost advantage of synthetic gems there is also the security of knowing that these gemstones are just about the most ethically sourced you can find. No 'Blood Diamonds', no funding genocidal wars, no questionable mining or other working conditions, no ecologically damaging extraction or production methods and no risk that child labour (or forced labour) is involved.

They are worth considering if you are one of the increasing number of people to whom these matters are top priority. In the end, it is down to personal preference. To some people, it is the look of a piece of jewellery which matters, not whether or not the stones came out of the ground, and to them, the lower cost is an added advantage. To others it is the mystery of the natural stone which captivates, for which they are prepared to pay a large premium and overlook the problem of supply.

Synthetic and cultured diamonds. Like cultured emeralds, which have been around since the 1930s, synthetic diamonds have also been around for a while. Originally used in industry, gem quality synthetic diamonds have been available to consumers since the 1980s. Like all synthetic gemstones, synthetic diamonds have the same physical, optical and chemical properties and they are as hard as natural stones (at 10 on the Mohs scale). They are essentially the same, but grown in a laboratory rather than in the ground, the biggest difference from natural stones being their price.

One extra benefit of synthetics is that the sourcing of these diamonds is completely and unequivocally ethical. There is no possibility of any suspect mining, employment or trading practices to worry about.

However, the processes for producing synthetic diamonds is a complex one, and the quality of the stones is very high, so they are only less expensive in comparison to high grade diamonds. They will often be more costly than a medium grade natural diamond.

Simulations and imitations

Now we've established what a created or cultured gemstone is, what is the difference between these laboratory grown gemstones, gemstone simulants and imitations?

Simulated stones 'simulate' the appearance of other stones, but they are not the same. They can be natural stones which look like the gemstone they 'simulate' or they can be imitations.

Two good examples of natural simulants of diamond are white sapphire and white zircon. White sapphire is a corundum, so it is the next hardest mineral after diamond. Although it can be mistaken for diamond by the layman, it does not have the same brilliance and has to be kept very clean of day to day grease and grime to retain its lustre. White zircon is fiery, but much softer than sapphire (at 6.5 to 7 on Mohs scale) and not really practical for daily wear as a stone in an engagement ring.

Imitation gems are simply made from clear or coloured glass, plastics or resins. Examples of imitations used in place of diamonds and other stones are Swarovski crystal, cubic zirconium (Cz) and what used to be known as 'paste'.

A note on moissanite

Moissanite has become a popular man-made simulant for diamond. Synthetic moissanite (silicon carbide) is produced in a near-colourless form and its brilliance is only slightly less than a natural diamond. It does however tend to have a slightly yellow or greenish-grey hue, although new developments are constantly improving the available colours. Moissanite is rated with a hardness of over 9 on Mohs scale, it displays excellent toughness and its durability can compete with diamond. However, I have found princess cut moissanite to be quite brittle at the corners and liable to break in a four-claw setting. This can also happen in diamond, but is much more likely with moissanite. At the moment, if you get the right colour and can avoid shapes with sharp corners, moissanite may be an acceptable option for some.

Conclusion

Laboratory grown, synthetic, cultured or created gemstones and diamonds are an ethical alternative to mined stones. All four terms and descriptions are commonly used.

It takes some time to grow the crystals for these gems and they are chemically, optically and physically identical to the stones which come out of the ground. They are also of very high quality and are less expensive than the same quality mined stones, although they are not cheap as their quality makes them comparable with the best mined stones.

They are not fake, imitation or simulated and are increasingly popular owing to their many benefits, not least the guarantee of ethical sourcing.

It is important to be properly advised when choosing laboratory grown gems to ensure you are getting them from a reputable source.

CHAPTER 11

WHICH METAL?

We've looked in some detail at the options available to you for the gemstone in your ring. Now it is time to think about the metals it could be made from.

The four precious metals most often used in jewellery are gold, platinum, palladium and silver. All metals used in jewellery are alloys, i.e. combinations of metals added to the precious metal to improve workability and hardness.

Summary

- Which metal you decide to use will depend on your aesthetic and your budget, and the colour which best suits the wearer

- Yellow gold is the simplest and most straightforward metal, the easiest to work and most traditional. An alternative is 'rose gold'

- Rose gold has a higher percentage of copper. It is as well to have a rose gold wedding ring made at the same time to ensure the same colour

- There are three principal options if you want a white metal. Platinum is the best but also the most expensive

- Hallmarking is your guarantee of quality. It is mandatory in the UK but not in the US, and online purchases may not be hallmarked. Beware of nickel in white metals purchased in the USA

- Fashions in ring metals change constantly. At the time of writing it is moving away from white metals to warm yellow and rose golds.

Precious metal alloys and qualities

For jewellery, each manufacturer and maker has their own closely guarded preferred alloy composition. There is constant development and experimentation to improve the characteristics of these alloys as the different combinations influence colour, durability, hardness, lustre and workability for both casting and forming.

Some alloy metals are more expensive than others. For example, 9ct white gold may be more expensive than 9ct yellow gold if the alloy in the former is palladium and it is plated with rhodium, whereas the alloy of the latter may be copper and other less precious metals.

It is important to note that the wedding band must be the same metal and metal quality as the engagement ring or one will wear the other away owing to the different hardness of different precious metal alloys.

A caution about nickel. A further caution about white metal alloys is about nickel. Nickel is a common allergen and causes contact dermatitis in about 10% of the population. Its use in jewellery in the EU is controlled (European Nickel Directive 1994) and most fine jewellery sold in the UK contains no nickel. This is not the case with jewellery from the USA. If you buy a white gold ring in the USA it is likely to contain nickel. When the rhodium plating wears off, as it will, the wearer can become sensitive to the nickel in a fairly short time scale and the ring will become unwearable. I have had to remount a number of rings completely for clients who have bought online and from the USA.

Hallmarking is a safeguard. All precious metals sold in the UK must be hallmarked as an independent guarantee of quality and purity. The hallmark will tell the consumer what percentage of alloy is included in the precious metal they are buying and ensure it does not contain any forbidden alloys.

It is the retailer's responsibility to ensure that the jewellery carries a UK or EU recognised hallmark, and it is illegal to sell precious metals in the UK without such a mark. In the USA and other countries hallmarking is not always required, and rings bought online may not be hallmarked, so it is more difficult for the consumer to be sure of the quality of the metal.

Gold

Gold for jewellery comes in different qualities, or carats, and sometimes in a range of colours, depending on the alloys used in making the final article.

In its un-alloyed state, gold is a highly sought-after precious yellow metal which, for thousands of years, has been used as currency, a visible symbol of wealth and self-adornment. Its chemical symbol is Au from the Latin aurum, meaning shining dawn.

Gold is found in igneous rocks and quartz veins, or in the form of nuggets and grains in river beds. The main mining areas are Africa, the USA, the former USSR, Canada, Australia and South America. 'Fair trade' and 'fair mined' gold is available in the UK.

Gold is dense, soft, shiny and the most malleable and ductile of the known metals. Pure gold is 24ct. The purity of commercially sold gold jewellery ranges from 9ct at the lower end through 14ct and 18ct to 22ct. Pure gold is too soft to be practical for jewellery.

Rose gold. Rose gold gets its characteristic pink hue from a higher percentage of copper in its alloy mix. The depth of colour will depend on the exact proportions of copper and other alloys, so one 9ct rose gold ring will not necessarily be identical in colour to another if they are made in different workshops. If you plan to have a rose gold engagement ring, it will be as well to consider making the wedding band at the same time, or at least by the same workshop, to ensure the colours match.

White gold. Gold is yellow. Lots of people assume that there is a special sort of gold which is white. Sadly, this is not the case. White gold is achieved by mixing yellow gold with white alloys, such as cobalt, zinc, palladium and platinum. Then it is finished by plating with rhodium, which is a shiny white and very expensive metal. The external white colour which you see is therefore rhodium and not gold. This is why there is no visible difference in the appearance of 9ct and 18ct white gold, unlike 9ct and 18ct yellow gold which are clearly different colours owing to the different proportions of yellow gold in the mix. In time, rhodium wears off the shank of a white gold ring, and it will have to be re-plated to keep it white and shiny.

Rhodium plating

This usually means that every two–three years, or perhaps even more frequently, the plating on both the wedding and engagement rings will need to be replaced. There are three considerations here.

Firstly, re-plating rings with rhodium is not cost-free, and if you are thinking of 18ct white gold instead of platinum in order to keep the costs down, you will spend the difference on re-plating within a short space of time.

Secondly, in order to re-plate a ring, all the old rhodium has to be removed. You do not just re-plate on top of the existing rhodium. This can cause additional wear to the metal in the ring, especially if it is done every couple of years, so if the shank is quite thin it might eventually have to be replaced altogether.

Thirdly, if you simply prefer the shiny white appearance of rhodium over the rather dull surface that platinum and palladium settle into in a short time, you may decide that it is worth the bother. If that is the case, consider 9ct white gold rather than 18ct. It is harder because it contains more alloy than 18ct, and the alloy is often palladium, a hard white platinum-group metal. A further advantage arises because 9ct gold is 37.5% gold and 62.5% white alloy, so it is therefore whiter than 18ct gold and the wear on the plating doesn't show up as much. This means it may need to be re-plated less often.

A plain white gold wedding band will show up the wear much more than a white gold engagement ring, and more quickly. The engagement ring will typically display wear on the inside of the hand where it is least noticeable, whereas the wedding ring turns constantly on the finger, so wear will be all around the band and be more visible.

In the past, when a white metal was required in jewellery, white gold was the only economical alternative to platinum, and it is much harder and more durable than silver. However, palladium now has its own hallmark and may be chosen as a cost effective and durable white metal alternative to platinum or white gold.

Platinum

Platinum is a naturally white metal so a platinum ring will never change in appearance (unlike white gold), and it is hard and strong. Because it is white, a platinum setting enhances the brilliance of diamonds and other gemstones so it is the best metal in which to set diamonds, but it is also the most expensive option. Along with palladium, it is generally used for the mount of diamonds in yellow or rose gold rings so that their colour is less influenced by reflected yellow or pinkish tints.

In the UK, platinum jewellery is typically hallmarked at 95% purity, making it purer even than 22ct gold (91.67%). The remaining 5% is made up of alloys which improve its workability.

Platinum is hypoallergenic, so is a good choice for anyone with metal sensitivities or allergies. With wear, it does lose its shine and will dull down very quickly to a light grey metal, which many people do not find attractive. So if you want a shiny white metal ring you may choose white gold instead or have your platinum plated with rhodium.

Palladium

Palladium has been used in jewellery for many years, most commonly as a mount for diamonds in a yellow gold ring, or as an alloy in platinum and white gold jewellery.

It is now used increasingly in its own right as a jewellery metal since receiving its own hallmark in 2009. It has become particularly popular as an alternative to platinum and white gold for reasons of both cost (similar to the cost of 14ct gold) and colour – it is another naturally white metal, but world supplies of palladium are limited and the cost has increased owing to its use in jewellery.

Platinum and palladium are very close to one another on the chemical periodic table and share many physical characteristics. Palladium jewellery is as pure as platinum, and is nearly as hard, but palladium is half the density of platinum so does feel much lighter on the hand, and may wear less well over the years. Like platinum, it loses its shine quickly, and it is a slightly greyer metal which is why it is more popular for men's wedding bands where a white metal is required. It is, however, used increasingly in engagement rings for both genders where budget is an issue.

One word of caution: palladium is difficult to work owing to its brittleness in manufacture. This is not a problem in wear, but it does mean that palladium rings can be more difficult to resize, and sometimes the solder line becomes visible, although this can be overcome by rhodium plating.

Silver

Silver jewellery is generally Sterling silver, which is 92.5% pure. It is much too soft a metal to use for a ring which is to be worn for a lifetime, and it is not hard enough or strong enough as a medium for setting diamonds, so it is not used for diamond engagement rings or any rings with precious stones. If you are considering silver on its own or set with a semi-precious stone like amethyst, do be aware that this ring will not last forever. It will need to be designed with a much heavier shank and setting, will become misshapen and the surface will look a bit battered within a few years.

Conclusion

Which metal you decide to use will depend on your aesthetic and your budget, and particularly on what colour best suits the wearer.

Yellow gold is the simplest and most straightforward metal. It has a warmth and richness unmatched by the white metals and has been a symbol of luxury for centuries. Rose gold is similarly warm, with a pinker tone.

If you want a white metal, the best option is platinum, as long as you accept its dull appearance or have it plated. If you want a shiny white, I would choose 9ct (not 18ct) white gold for the reasons I have given above. If it is simply a budget matter and not one of aesthetics, palladium is another alternative to platinum because it is the nearest in appearance and qualities.

Although white metals took over the fashion for engagement rings in recent years, it rather looks as though this is changing yet again with a resurgence in popularity of yellow and even rose gold.

So whichever you choose, fashions change. Think more about which colour will suit the wearer rather than what is currently in vogue.

CHAPTER 12

CHOOSING THE SHAPE OF YOUR STONE

Diamonds and gemstones come in a surprisingly wide range of shapes, sizes and proportions, and some work better than others, especially in a ring. There is a lot to be said for choosing one of the less common shapes for your ring as it will enhance the more personal nature of the design.

Better quality and larger size precious stones will be cut to maximise their beauty and carat weight rather than to fit to standard sizes. So your ring should be made around your gem, rather than the gem supplied to fit a standard ring mount.

Summary

- There is a wide range of shapes available for both diamonds and gemstones

- Shape and cut are intimately linked, and the quality of cut influences the desirability and price of a stone

- Shapes with pointed corners can be damaged in claw settings, and you should avoid round stones with a 'culet' at the point

- Simpler cuts often require higher grade and more expensive stones

- Older stone cuts and shapes can be difficult to match, and less popular shapes can be difficult to source.

Shape and cut

There are twelve principle shapes for diamonds and fifteen principle shapes for gemstones. Shape and cut are separate elements but are linked – a shape can determine which cuts are possible, but there may be more than one cut suitable to a shape. For example, a square shaped stone may be 'princess' cut or stepped. The former is sparklier as there are more facets to the princess cut.

Among diamond and gemstone shapes there is obviously a great deal of overlap, but there are differences in the way gemstones and diamonds are cut, and a distinction is sometimes made between 'faceted', which is a standard gemstone cut, and 'diamond cut' as a term applied to gemstones. Diamond cut tends to be a brighter cut for the stone as it involves more facets and more cutting. Not all gemstones are suitable for this treatment as some are either too brittle or too soft to withstand the extra pressure and work it involves.

The less popular or less common shapes can be difficult to source when you want a particular stone, so it may be a case of 'first catch your gemstone'. As long as you allow time in your design process nothing is impossible as stones can be specially cut to order from the rough.

Gemstone shapes

Points to note

There are some things you should consider when choosing the shape of your diamond or gemstone. Stones with pointed corners, like square cuts, marquise and pear shapes, can be fragile at the points. This is one reason why re-setting old jewellery can be problematic.

Three of these shapes are also the most difficult to set in claws in a visually pleasing way because of the problem of positioning the claws such that they hold the stone securely but do not materially change the whole look of the piece.

Claw-set pear, heart and marquise stones

Bezel setting (Chapter 13) is a good alternative for these shapes as long as it is designed to maximise the amount of light entering the stone. Bezels also protect the edges of brittle and soft stones.

Diamond shapes

If we start with diamonds, the most popular shape is obviously the round brilliant cut. There are also 'modified brilliant cuts' where brilliant cut faceting is applied to different shapes of stone. This group includes oval, marquise, heart, pear-shape, radiant cut (relatively new), trillion (triangle), and antique cushion cut (rectangular or square with rounded corners).

Other shapes include the emerald cut, a simpler cut originally devised for softer, more brittle emeralds, and the baguette cut, including the tapered trapezoid baguette. This latter is another very simple cut with few facets which is generally used for side stones. Both emerald and baguette cuts require higher quality diamonds; because they have fewer facets and are less 'brilliant' in appearance, any inclusions are much easier to see, so stones with few obvious facets tend to be selected for these cuts. This can make them more expensive per carat on average than other options.

The Asscher cut is another traditional cut for diamonds. Sophisticated and less common than many of the other rectangular shapes, it has a few more facets than the emerald cut, and is usually used for a more 'square' shape.

Finally, the princess cut is the square stone with pointy corners which has a lot of facets and high brilliance. It is a popular shape, but it is worth bearing in mind that, although diamond is the hardest mineral known to man, it can be brittle and is not indestructible.

I have seen princess cut diamonds which have been damaged in the corners when being claw-set. This damage is not immediately apparent until the time comes to reset the stones, or even just to repair the inevitable wear on a ring which is worn daily. Dismounting the stones to perform this work reveals the cracks or chips in the diamond corners, so you cannot always know whether any stone is in good enough condition to remount until it is removed from its setting.

Old fashioned diamond cuts. There are older diamond cuts including the 'rose' cut, Mazarin and 'old European'. These have been superseded and are rarely produced now because they have a much lower level of brilliance than modern cuts. They have their own charm and attractions, but are very difficult to match if you are trying to remount inherited jewellery. Older stones were almost always hand cut, and this inevitably limited what could be done with the stone.

Gemstone shapes

In gemstones, a round simply 'faceted' stone isn't cut the same way as a diamond, and generally has fewer facets than the brilliant cut. This is also true of the oval, pear-shape, marquise, heart, antique cushion, triangle or trillion. Most of these cuts have fewer facets than diamonds of the same shape would have. Emerald and baguette cuts, as well as the Asscher, are simpler and so usually the same as for diamonds, and the square cut is very similar to the princess cut.

There is also the 'antique square cushion' cut which has checker-board faceting on the top of the stone, and a 'cushion' cut, which is similar to the emerald cut. Unlike the emerald cut, which is actually octagonal, this doesn't have its corners cut off.

Parts of a gemstone

There are some basic terms that it might be useful for you to know when people talk about different parts of the gemstone. Take a look at this diagram of a typical brilliant cut stone.

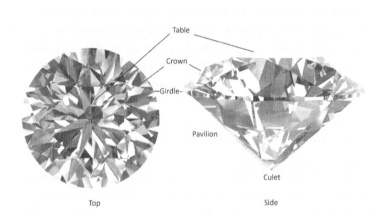

Parts of a faceted gemstone

The flat top of the stone is called the table, the widest part is the girdle, and right at the bottom, you have what is known as the 'culet' (pronounced 'kewlet'). This was originally introduced for round cuts to protect the bottom of the stone, and it does still appear in modern cut diamonds. Viewed from the top through the table, it may be visible in some clear stones, especially larger diamonds, as a dead or 'black' spot, not reflecting back as much light as the surrounding faceting. Generally speaking a culet is not desirable in a well cut diamond. If your diamond certificate indicates that a culet is present, you should view the stone before having it set in a ring.

The whole area above the girdle is called the 'crown'. Below the girdle is the 'pavilion'. There are different types of facet, depending on the cut, between the girdle and the flat top of the table on one hand, and between the girdle and the bottom of the stone on the other. The way in which these facets are cut will affect the brilliance of the stone.

The ratio of width to depth of any stone will impact on its brilliance because of the way the light comes into the stone and is reflected back out of it. This is discussed in more detail in Chapter 8.

Conclusion

The quality of cut of any gemstone is an important element in assessing its overall suitability, desirability and price. There is a surprisingly wide range of stone shapes available, and some are more suited to rings than others. The more uncommon the shape you choose, the more personal will be your ring, providing the shape of the stone does not compromise the integrity, beauty and practicality of the design.

The setting should be designed to protect vulnerable stone shapes as some with pointed corners can be damaged in claw settings, and you should try to avoid round stones with a 'culet'.

The shape and cut are intimately linked and the simpler cuts often require higher grade and more expensive stones. There is a clear relationship between the depth of cut and the brilliance of a stone owing to the way light is reflected within the stone. This is particularly an issue with diamonds, less so with coloured stones, and is one of the determinants of diamond quality and price.

Older stone cuts and shapes can be more difficult to match when remodelling old jewellery, and less popular shapes can be difficult to source in any given coloured gemstone specification. So getting the colour, quality and shape combination you want in a pink sapphire, for example, may take a little while.

As long as you allow time to source your stone or perhaps have it cut to order, anything is possible, and it is often worth waiting for just the right stone as this will make all the difference to your ring.

CHAPTER 13

RING STYLES AND
DESIGN FEATURES

There is a lot to think about when creating a design for your ring. With a wide range of styles, settings, mounts, shank or band profiles and design features, there is great potential for variation. Each feature of your ring design has to work well with the others to create a robust and pleasing ring. I don't want to confuse you with too much information, but you will come across these elements and it is as well to know what they mean and what their pros and cons may be.

Summary

- Think of the engagement ring and the wedding band at the same time. Many engagement ring designs will not work with a straight wedding band

- A good ring design will combine a suitable setting and the desired design features into a pleasing and wearable mount for your stones

- Think about the practicalities of daily wear. Your designer should pay close attention to all these elements to make sure you get the ring design which will work for her and which you will both love.

Think about the wedding band

Do not be carried away by the elegance of a ring design without thinking about how it will work with the wedding band.

One thing which is rarely considered when choosing an engagement ring is how the wedding band will lie against it. If the stones are wider than the band and the design does not take this into account, you may have to have a shaped wedding band or accept a gap between the two rings.

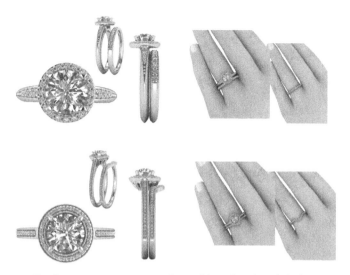

Designs to accompany a shaped band and a plain band

Alternatively, some designs will sit on top of a plain wide wedding band with a thin cross-section.

Some people don't object to a gap, and many do not want a shaped band as it often looks odd when it is worn on its own.

Most jewellers who want to sell you a ring from their stock will not mention this. It is not in their interest to create questions in your mind, and it is not a consideration that would enter most people's heads either. Be aware of the potential for more expense because shaped bands have to be made to fit and will cost more than a straight band, especially if they are diamond-set.

Styles

The six styles you will see most often are: solitaire, three stone or trilogy, five stone, halo, cluster and band. Let's tackle them in turn.

Solitaire. This describes a single stone ring of any shape. The most basic form is a round brilliant-cut diamond 4-claw or 6-claw solitaire.

Solitaires – 4 claw and 6 claw

This may be a good choice for the minimalist. For the more adventurous and individual there are plenty of potential variations on the theme.

Solitaire – alternative settings

The 4-claw 'NSEW' looks very pretty, but it will require a shaped wedding band to fit around it, as will some basket settings and bezels.

| NSEW | Bezel | Basket |

Solitaire settings with shaped bands – NSEW, basket, bezel

Trilogy. Another classic is the three stone trilogy ring. This has a central stone which is usually, but not always, larger than the two matching side stones. Again, any shape or type of stone can be used, and this style often incorporates a coloured gemstone as the centre stone. As a gemstone may be less expensive than a similar size and quality of diamond, you may be able to use a larger stone within your budget than if the ring were all diamonds. Do be careful about choosing the setting for a trilogy if you want to be able to wear a straight wedding band with it.

Trilogy rings

Five-stone. For engagement rings, this design is less common now than it used to be, and less popular than the trilogy. Similar pros and cons apply, and it may be most suited to a larger finger, keeping the ring in scale with the personality yet still within budget.

Five stone rings

Halo. In recent years this has become a very popular choice for engagement rings. It enables you to get maximum impact for less money. You can use a small central diamond or gemstone with lots of small diamonds in the halo, or you can use a larger central stone and enhance it with the halo. The central stone can be either claw-set or bezel-set. If it is claw-set, take note of the appearance of the space between the centre stone and the surrounding halo. A well designed ring will minimise the appearance of this gap.

Single and double halos

Depending on the setting, you will need to be aware of the potential for a shaped wedding band to go with this ring. If you are on a tight budget, do not save on this ring only to find yourself paying a lot more when it comes to the next stage.

Cluster. The halo and cluster are similar, but have key design differences. While the halo is contained in a channel surrounding the central stone, a cluster is a collection of claw-set stones where the setting of each stone is connected to its neighbour.

Cluster with shaped and with straight band

This design in particular is one where it may be necessary to have a shaped wedding band, or have it sit on top of a wide plain one with a thin cross-section.

Band. Some people choose a simpler stone-set band for their engagement rather than a ring with feature diamonds or gemstones. This is an obvious choice for a man's engagement ring.

Diamond bands

Because there is nothing to catch or knock, it may also be suitable for someone who is very active, for healthcare professionals or those who cannot wear one of the other designs at work.

Combined wedding/engagement ring with tulip design

This is a design for a combined wedding and engagement ring which I created for a client who wanted her ring to be simple, easy to wear, yet unique to her, and especially to remind her of her grandmother. It incorporates five small princess-cut channel-set diamonds and an applied design of stylised tulips – her grandmother's favourite flowers.

Freestyle. Of course there are many more options for your ring design, and, if you have it designed for you or design it yourself, you can create the most individual and personal ring. These are just a few of the more unusual engagement rings I have designed for clients.

Freestyle rings

Settings

The terms 'setting' and 'mount' are often interchangeable. Here, I define setting as the way stones are held in place. Mounts are more a sub-set of style but fit here because the same mount can be used in more than one style.

Claw set. Claws are the thin strips of metal which hold stones in place in the vast majority of rings. They can be different shapes and add to the design features. In ready-made rings, claws are usually round.

Platinum claws can be finer than gold claws because platinum is stronger and more hard-wearing than gold. In time, claws will need to be repaired or 'tipped'. Claw setting allows the maximum amount of light into the stone, which is one reason why it is so popular. It is also more forgiving than a bezel on stones which have poor symmetry or are less regular in shape. A common mistake in setting large stones is to use too few claws to keep the stone fixed in place without movement. The illustration shows a large stone in its original 4-claw setting which was not secure, and as remodelled to integrate the shoulders as a third set of claws.

Making a claw setting secure

One downside of a claw setting is that the claws will catch on fine fabrics such as tights or stockings, silk scarves and knitwear, often damaging the clothing. It is also possible to knock the ring and either damage the edges of the stone or push the claws out of alignment, loosening the stone.

Bezel set. A bezel setting is a ring of metal surrounding the stone. This can encase the whole stone or be a band around the girdle. A half-bezel has part of the bezel cut away at each side. The bezel can also be pierced to allow more light into the back of the stone. Depending on how much of the lower part of the stone the bezel covers, this style of setting does restrict the light entering the stone and can diminish the brilliance of a diamond or enhance the depth of colour of a gemstone.

Bezels

This setting has the advantage that it is smooth and gives a contemporary feel to some designs. It is very secure and difficult to damage, protects the stone, particularly more brittle gems like emerald, and won't catch on clothing as claws do.

Bar and tension set. A bar setting is a type of tension setting. This is where the stone is held under tension between two metal surfaces. It is a very contemporary look.

Bar and tension settings

As long as the stone is firmly anchored in the wall of the setting and there is metal to 'tie' the two surfaces together, it is pretty secure and offers some protection to the edges of the stone. If there is no 'tie' between the metal surfaces, then the design has to be very rigid to ensure that the stone does not come loose. These settings work best for rectangular stones where there is greater surface area contact.

Channel and grain set. Channel settings are mostly used to set stones in the side of the shank and in bands. It is the most secure setting for this purpose.

Channel and grain settings

The stones sit inside a channel in the band and a small amount of metal covers the edge of the stone. This keeps the stones in place and protects them from mechanical damage. Channel setting is particularly good for princess cut and baguette shank stones as it gives a smooth continuous finish.

If the channel also has little claws, it is a grain setting. In the latter, sometimes the grains hold the stones in place rather than the channel. At other times, both do the holding. This is particularly good for round stones as the grains fill the gaps between the stones

Pavé set. A pavé setting is, literally, like a 'pavement' of little stones all held in place by tiny claws or grains which are shared between neighbouring stones.

Pavé setting

It is more common as a setting for dress rings. Done well it will last a long time, but a lot of pavé settings are not very secure and it is easy to lose stones.

Rub-over or 'gypsy' set. This is where a stone is individually set directly into a hole made in the metal of the band. It is mostly used for small stones and does restrict the light entering the stone.

'Gypsy' setting

Composites. Composite settings group lots of small stones together to make them look like one larger stone. The idea is to give the appearance of, say, a 1.0ct diamond at a significantly lower cost, but they are not very convincing and can look a bit cheap. They are usually bezel-set to provide more stability to the illusion. If princess cut stones are used, these can be set flush against each other. Round stones will require claws between them.

Composite set stones

Mounts

Mounts – weave, basket, bypass, cathedral

Weave. A weave mount is a pretty claw setting which tapers as it nears the finger and so can allow you to wear a straight band even if you have a group of larger stones. This is particularly useful for trilogy rings.

Basket. The basket mount is a standard traditional mount and is often used with rectangular and large stones. It is solid and secure, but can be rather clunky and will be difficult to fit with a straight wedding band.

Bypass. The sweeping curves of a bypass mount are very attractive, rather like the 'NSEW' solitaire, but it has the same drawback in that a shaped wedding band is almost unavoidable.

Cathedral. The term 'cathedral' describes the way the shank rises at the point where it meets the central stone in a solitaire. It is reminiscent of the flying buttresses on, for example, Notre Dame Cathedral.

Shank shapes

The shape of the shank will, in part, be determined by the demands of the design, and in part on consideration of comfort of fit.

In general, a shank with an internal curve is more comfortable to wear and any good designer will maximise the comfort of your preferred design. This will depend on a variety of factors including band and design width, thickness, finger size and other rings which may be worn adjacent to the engagement ring.

Design features

To keep this as clear as possible, I have separated design features from style. All of these features could be applied to any style, and you can even combine more than one feature in your ring. But we'll take them one by one.

Shank stones

Shank stones and settings

These are the little stones which are set in the shank (or band) of the ring, usually at each side of the main setting. Generally shank stones will be round, square or baguette. They can be set in a channel, in claws or be grain set (also known as bead set). Channel and grain-set shank stones are the most secure.

Milgrain

Milgrain

Milgrain is a fine beading applied to the edges of rings and around halos or bezels. It gives a more decorative vintage feel to a ring so is used on 'modern vintage' designs, and works well on new wedding bands made to wear with a vintage engagement ring.

Filigree

Filigree

Filigree is the pierced design found on many vintage and vintage-style rings. The only problem with filigree rings is the ease with which dirt and grease can get trapped in the design, so it is especially important to keep these rings cleaned.

Moulded and incised or engraved designs

Moulded features

A moulded design is applied on top of the shank. If you like the look of mixed metals, such as yellow gold and platinum together, this can make an attractive feature. If it is properly done, the design will not abrade adjacent fingers. You may want a wedding band to match so that they work as a pair. If so, I would strongly recommend that these be made together.

An incised or engraved design cuts into the metal rather than sitting on top of it. It can either be engraved by hand or be created during the casting process. Hand engraving is very skilled specialist work and can be expensive. Your designer will use an experienced craftsperson for this work and it is likely to add to the time it takes to make the ring. If you want the wedding band to match, have this done at the same time.

Conclusion

There is a lot to think about when it comes to the design of your perfect ring, but don't feel overwhelmed by it all. A good designer will start with the look you are trying to achieve and the information you can provide about the person for whom you are creating it. He or she will use the best combination of style, features, settings and mount to realise that vision.

If you are buying a ready-made ring, don't just think about the look of the ring. Give thought to the practicalities of daily wear and think ahead to the wedding band.

CHAPTER 14

SOME GREAT PROPOSAL STORIES

I have included these proposal stories because I think they are inspiring, if occasionally Byzantine in their complexity and organisation.

There are so many ways you can make the event one to remember and regale your grandchildren with. Some stories are as reported and others are written directly by the participants. I have kept the latter as they are as I feel it adds something of the excitement and immediacy of their feeling for the event.

I just love this proposal story, for all sorts of reasons.

The Story of Ruth and Arjan

Engaged Easter Sunday 2013, Married Sept 2014.

Easter is Ruth's favourite time of year. Arjan had created an Easter Egg hunt for Ruth and her son, who was just five at the time. He'd written up loads of clues that started in their garden, then sent her by car to her parents' garden and finally back to their own.

The final clue sent Ruth and her son to a wooded area at the bottom of the garden where they had to dig down into a huge pile of leaves. There they found a bag with two Easter eggs in it, both addressed to Ruth. One was a 'Hotel Chocolat' Easter egg in a big box all beautifully wrapped and ribboned. The other was one of those little eggs in red and gold foil with ducks on that you'll find in any sweet shop.

Arjan told Ruth that she had to choose which egg she wanted. Naturally, Ruth wanted the big, beautiful, gorgeously wrapped Easter egg, but she noticed that the little ordinary egg had a sticker on the bottom that said 'open me carefully', so she chose the little egg.

When she opened it, there was cotton wool inside and, in that, her engagement ring. At that point, Arjan got down on his knee and proposed.

Ruth said it was really special because her son was there too. He was thrilled, dancing around saying, 'Wow, Mummy, that's lovely', and was involved in the whole thing. It was a proposal which included all three of them.

When Ruth and Arjan got married in the local church, they had a marquee in the garden, her mum did the catering, and it was a lovely relaxed family day.

Ruth said that they had previously gone out looking for rings. She'd seen one she liked, but they wanted platinum (it was gold) and she was going to have to wait eight weeks to have it made. So she wasn't expecting Arjan to propose so soon. He'd returned to the shop and asked to have the ring to propose with, and planned to arrange to have the same ring made in platinum. When it came to it, Ruth didn't want to part with the ring which Arjan had proposed with as it had a special meaning and significance to her, so she kept the white gold ring and that is what she wears now.

Marcus used Aneta's birthday as a way to cover up the elaborate arrangements he made for his proposal. He loved the whole process of creating the event for her, and I think that comes across in this story which is exactly as he told it to me.

The Story of Marcus and Aneta

'Aneta and I got engaged in August 2014. We booked a holiday in Mexico to celebrate Aneta's birthday which meant my surprise proposal could go under the radar without Aneta realising what was going to happen.

'Before we arrived in Mexico I was emailing our hotel, organising everything to the last detail as this was the most important thing I had ever done! But first I needed a ring so did some research to design my own ring and had it made in good time. It was perfect.

'So we begin our journey to Mexico, the ring is hidden in my suitcase and I'm nervous in case they see it at customs and want to search the case, spoiling the surprise. But everything goes smoothly. We arrive at the hotel in Riviera Maya and it is incredible.

'So now I need to prepare and get everything sorted. I make excuses to Aneta so I can sneak off and finish the arrangements without her realising. I have planned everything to be done on her birthday. We wake to a beautiful bouquet of flowers left at our door, and at breakfast the waiters sing "Happy Birthday". The day is going perfectly. We spend it on the beach in the beautiful sunshine until lunch, and again the waiters sing "Happy Birthday". Aneta loves it.

'We stroll along the beach with cocktails, talking and laughing about the four wonderful years we have spent together. As the sunset begins I surprise her with a sunset couple massage looking out to the beautiful ocean, followed by a glass of champagne – so romantic. We head back to our room to change for dinner. There is a knock at the door – the hotel has sent a nice bottle of bubbly. Perfect. Aneta is loving our day, as I get nervous!

'We stroll along the seafront to where I have organised a surprise dinner on the beach. Everything has been organised with the waiters – at the end of the meal they are to bring out the ring in a cake made by the hotel in the shape of a ring box. We finish the beautiful food; it's going amazingly. The waiter then blindfolds Aneta and a man starts to play "Lady in Red" on a saxophone. As they bring out the ring, Aneta bursts out crying with happiness and says yes. And we dance under the moonlight. The absolute best day of our lives.'

Rafael and William's story is one of a whirlwind romance, and another where a birthday served as cover for all the arrangements. This one is less elaborate but was the perfect memorable day for them both.

The Story of Rafael and William

Rafael is Brazilian. He came to London to learn English, set up a successful business and stayed. William is English and shy.

One week after they met, they decided that this was a serious relationship and they were going to stay together. Two and a half months later Rafael proposed, and they were married a short time afterwards. This is how it happened.

It was William's birthday, so, under the cloak of birthday celebrations, they flew to Paris where Rafael booked a table for lunch in the Michelin starred Jules Verne restaurant at the top of the Eiffel Tower. He had alerted the Maître d' to his plans.

They had a wonderful meal with staggering views over Paris. At the end of the meal, the waiter brought a huge silver salver with a high domed cover, announced it was their dessert and, with a small bow to them both, left it on the table.

Rafael lifted the cover. Under it was a beautiful cake with two gold rings arranged on top. Rafael then got down on one knee and asked William to marry him.

It took William a full minute to answer, he was so overcome, by which time other people in the restaurant realised what was happening and got up to applaud. Luckily William finally said yes and the restaurant brought two glasses of champagne over. They spent the rest of the day in blissful happiness wandering around Paris.

The lengths to which some chaps will go to surprise and delight their fiancée. For Byzantine, this almost takes the cake, but it just shows that all we really want is a lovely, thoughtful surprise. And Steve was pretty pleased with himself too.

The Story of Steve and Rachel

'I proposed to Rachel in May 2015.

'I told her that the directors of my parent company were holding a shareholders' meeting in Reims, Champagne (somewhere she'd been wanting to go for a while) and that they wanted me to attend. Wives and girlfriends were invited for the Saturday night.

'I contacted her boss secretly and asked if she could have the Monday off work so we could really stay two nights.

'I told her that the others were hiring cars and that I'd hire us a car too and drive down via the Eurotunnel. I said that I'd picked a cool car, but it was a surprise.

'We picked the car up on Saturday morning – a Nissan Figaro (her favourite car). She thought I was just being thoughtful, and luckily didn't suspect anything.

'At one point she said, "Well that's two things ticked off my list: going to Champagne and driving a Figaro".

'My business partner was in on it, and I had him call me whilst I was driving so that Rachel answered. He said a few things to her and that we were meeting at the restaurant at eight to eat at 8.30, as requested.

'We got to the guest house a little late, but it was a really nice place with just five bedrooms on a champagne farm in a quiet little village called Vrigny outside of Reims.

'The receptionist at the guest house knew what was happening and not to say that we were booked in for two nights. She also gave us a bottle of champagne from the farm and gave me a little wink when we arrived!

'We got a taxi to take us to the Michelin star restaurant, and when we arrived, it was an amazing old chateau in beautiful grounds. There was ivy growing all over the house and a classic Ferrari parked outside.

'Rach got out of the taxi and said, "This is like a fairly-tale" – still none the wiser.

'I had booked the table under my business partner's name, and called the day before to tell the waiters what I was planning and arrange that they would take us out to a private table on the terrace and bring over a bottle of champagne, which they did perfectly to plan.

'At this point, when there was nobody there, Rach was wondering where everybody was and was worried we were in the wrong place, but I just said they must be running a bit late and not to worry.

'I then told her I'd put together a photo album on my phone of all the things that we'd done together over the years and started showing her all the pictures. She thought it was a very nice thing to do, but was still none the wiser.

'I then asked her if she was ready to tick another thing off her list and reminded her of the times she used to drag me past a shop window when I visited her in Liverpool. At that point she realised I was talking about a jewellery shop and she went silent and started to fill up.

'I pulled out the ring box and got down on one knee, said a few words and asked her to marry me. After a few seconds of complete shock, and lots of tears, she said yes and gave me a hug.

'At that point another table of guests had obviously noticed what was happening and cheered, then came over with some tissues for Rach and took a few pictures.

'I also told her nobody else was coming, this was all for her, and she'd got Monday off work so we could go champagne tasting the following day, which came as almost as big a shock to her as the question itself.

'We sat outside for about forty-five minutes whilst she calmed down and stopped crying. She had mascara all over the place; it was a great hour or so out there.

'I was a bit worried about whether she would like the ring or not, but she absolutely loved it. She said all she'd really wanted was to be surprised, but didn't think I'd be able to do it. Every time we went away, everybody would say to her "Do you think he's going to pop the question this time?", but somehow I managed to get her all the way out to a nice restaurant in Champagne, in her favourite car, without her suspecting a thing. Very pleased with myself, and happy she said yes, of course!'

The story of Daniel and Aléna

It was the anniversary of their first year together and, not a man to hang about, Daniel had decided to ask Aléna to marry him. He wanted it to be a really memorable surprise and, in true Dan-fashion, a bit of a tease too. So this was all arranged under the guise of celebrating their 'first anniversary'.

Dan booked a nice boutique hotel on Lake Garda and told Aléna he hadn't been able to get *anything* on Lake Como. They had a lovely couple of days in Lake Garda, but on the third day he told Aléna that 'the hotel' was transferring them to a sister hotel on Lake Como owing to a 'problem with the kitchens' – for Health and Safety reasons they would have to move and they were booked into this hotel on Lake Como.

Despite her protests they packed their bags and drove off. On the journey Dan gave Aléna the Trip Advisor details for the new hotel, 'edited' with a new name, pictures and awful reviews, crucially keeping the address the same. She read 'no hot water, bad food etc' so was feeling really miserable. But they continued to follow directions to the hotel and arrived outside the Grand Hotel Tremezzo – a gorgeous, five-star luxury hotel on Lake Como.

Against more protests Dan insisted they go ask for directions to this 'other place'. Aléna really didn't want to go in because this was so beautiful, and where they were going would be even more of a let down by comparison. Dan told Aléna that these old historic hotels were so big they wouldn't know better if he said they had a booking, and if they had a room free they would just give it to them, so they might as well try. The clerk looked up Dan's name up on the computer and said, 'Yes sir, your room is ready for you.' Dan just said there must be someone else with the same name. But when they got to the fabulous room he had arranged, the penny finally dropped and she realised he'd planned it all along!

They had a wonderful dinner on the terrace overlooking the lake, with a full moon (also specially ordered), and Dan suggested they take dessert in their room. Dan ordered and called Aléna onto the balcony as there was 'something he wanted to show her'.

He told her a story about a 19-year old woman and a 21-year old man who met at a dance. He was an electrician and she was a catering assistant and pretty quickly they decided to get married. These were Dan's grandparents.

Then Dan took out a box. 'Here's the ring my grandmother wore all her life, they were young and it was all they could afford back then, but it has very special sentimental value. So I thought it was appropriate to have it with me when I asked the question.'

Then he got down on one knee, asked Aléna, and of course she said yes.

There's a lovely postscript to this story. When they returned to London, they did the usual tour of Boodles et al, looking for Aléna's ring. In each shop the assistant brought out four or five rings for Aléna to look at, but without success. Then they found this tiny boutique where a little old French lady talked to them for a while before asking Aléna to tell her what she had in mind. The French lady disappeared and came back with just *one* ring, and for Alèna it was the perfect ring. The French lady simply said, 'I knew it would be.'

CHAPTER 15

GOOD LUCK!

I hope you've found this book useful and informative and that it has shed new light on the whole process of finding the perfect engagement ring for the one you love. I'd be thrilled if it has also opened up options you had not yet considered and raised questions about the impact your choices can make.

And, as for originality, I believe that there is far too much mediocrity in this world and often despair of the creeping standardisation that global business inevitably brings to some important areas of our personal lives.

We all buy into it at some level, and mass production and standardisation certainly have their place – where would modern civilisation be without them? They also bring real advances to a wider community, making a positive impact on their lives. Mobile phone technology in Africa is one such fantastic resource which has changed the lives of poor farmers and would not have been possible without mass production.

But your personal token of love and commitment should be just that: personal and individual. No standard mass produced ring can do that job as well as a ring you have helped to design for her alone.

Starting a new life together is the beginning of an exciting adventure. However you go about making that most important of all proposals, I hope it will be with a ring she will value and love forever, as she will you.

GLOSSARY

4Cs – a method devised by the GIA and popularised by De Beers for classifying the Colour, Cut, Clarity and Carat Weight of diamonds

AGSL – American Gemmological Society Laboratories – a certifying body for diamonds

ARM – Alliance for Responsible Mining – www.responsiblemines.org

Band – also shank - the part of the ring which goes around the finger

Bezel – means of holding a gemstone in place in a setting using a continuous wire to surround the girdle of the stone

CAD – Computer Aided Design – software used to design a ring and illustrate the design to the client

CAM – Computer Aided Manufacture – programmed hardware which creates the ring model by interpreting 2-D CAM designs into 3-D waxes

Carat – ct/kt – has two meanings. The first describes the proportion of gold in an alloy - 24ct gold is 100% gold, so 18ct is 18/24ths or 75% gold. The second is a measurement of weight for gemstones – 1.0ct is approximately equal to 0.2g.

Claw – means of holding a gemstone in place in a setting using individual wires positioned around the stone

DDII – Diamond Development Initiative International – www.ddiiglobal.org

EGL – European Gemmological Laboratories - the name for a number of different certifying bodies for diamonds. Each EGL company is independent, so although they share a name EGL USA is not the same organisation as EGL Israel for example

Facets – the cut faces of a gemstone

Fluorescence – the natural tendency of some diamonds to fluoresce when exposed to ultra-violet light

GIA – Gemmological Institute of America – the oldest certifying body for diamonds

Girdle – the widest part of a gemstone where the top facets meet the bottom facets

HRD – Hoge Raad Voor Diamant (Diamond High Council,

Belgium) – certifying body for diamonds

IGI – International Gemmological Institute – certifying body for diamonds

KP or KPCS – Kimberley Process Certification Scheme – a now discredited system for certifying the source of rough diamonds

Mohs scale – a logarithmic scale describing the hardness of minerals from the hardest at 10 (diamond) down to the softest at 1 (talc)

NGO- Non-Governmental Organisation

Shank – also band – the part of the ring which goes around the finger

Shoulder – where the band or shank joins the gemstone setting

FURTHER INFORMATION

AGSL – American Gemmological Society Laboratories
www.americangemsociety.org

ARM – Alliance for Responsible Mining
www.responsiblemines.org

DDII – Diamond Development Initiative International
www.ddiiglobal.org

GIA – Gemmological Institute of America
www.gia.edu

Global Witness
www.globalwitness.org/campaigns/conflict-diamonds

RJC – Responsible Jewellery Council
www.responsiblejewellery.com

Nickel allergy and nickel release
www.assayoffice.co.uk/analytical-services/nickel-testing

Fair Trade Gold

www.fairtrade.org.uk/en/buying-fairtrade/gold

Fair Mined Gold

www.fairmined.org; fairgold.org

FREE RESOURCES
TO HELP YOU

If you need more information or help here are some resources which you can download or obtain directly from the Julie Peel website. More will be added as they are developed.

'What's her Style?' checklist – www.juliepeel.co.uk/Downloads/HerStyle

To estimate ring size – www.juliepeel.co.uk/downloads/ringsizetools

To receive a free ring sizing gadget by post quote 'BOOK1' – *include a postal address* – to email info@juliepeel.co.uk

For information on choosing a wedding ring and other useful topics see all the available materials and brochures at http://www.juliepeel.co.uk/JP-downloads

Alternatively, sign up for one of Julie's regular free live webinars and put your questions in person – see website for details: www.juliepeel.co.uk

ACKNOWLEDGEMENTS

A book is never written by one person alone, so grateful thanks to all of you for your help and support:

Nick Fitzhugh for detailed notes and comments – this is an altogether more concise and better book than it would otherwise have been, a service above and beyond the call of friendship.

Cressida Peever who read my first draft, removed many solecisms and spared my blushes.

For permission to use their inspiring stories – Steven Oddy, Rafael dos Santos, Ruth Buschman and Marcus Imrie.

For moral support and encouragement – my friends Grant Linscott, Caro Crawford, Jackie Marshall, Juan Lopez and Steven May.

All my clients, past and present, who have sought advice and allowed me to help them create such an important piece of jewellery. Without you there would have been nothing to write about.

And this book would never even have been a twinkle in my eye had it not been for the inspiration of Daniel and Andrew Priestley and Lucy McCarraher.

My especial thanks go to Andy Laughton for always being there and helping me make it this far in everything I do, and to Lucy Ellor who not only provided some of the gemmological background, but has worked with me for more years than either of us care to remember. Throughout those years she has been irreplaceable and the greatest support in bad times as well as good.

It just remains to mention Hannah, and she will know why.

THE AUTHOR

Julie Peel has been designing jewellery since 1998 and has more than seventeen years' experience in jewellery retail. Her passion is to create designs for women who do not want to follow the brand herds, who wear their jewellery as an expression their individual personality, and who care about where their jewellery comes from.

She now specialises in the design and creation of bespoke rings, but in her previous lives she was an academic, worked in overseas development in South America and in the UK charity sector. Her experience in these roles, her values and ethics, inform all her business practices.

Because she does not come from a traditional jewellery background, Julie perceives the jewellery industry from the viewpoint of a critical outsider, but with the contacts and knowledge of the insider. This leaves her uniquely placed to educate and inform her clients, and to arm them with the knowledge they need to make the best decisions for *them*. Hundreds of happy clients refer their friends and share with family, friends and strangers the story of their engagement ring.

Julie lives in London but travels the world in search of inspiration and glorious gems.

Contact details for Julie Peel:

Email – info@juliepeel.co.uk

Website – www.juliepeel.co.uk

Skype – juliedpeel

Facebook – JuliePeelBespoke

Twitter – @JuliePeelJewels

LinkedIn – uk.linkedin.com/in/juliedpeel

Pinterest – juliepeeljewels

Lightning Source UK Ltd.
Milton Keynes UK
UKOW07f0246170216

268533UK00009B/29/P